Crete

- A  in the text denotes a highly recommended sight
- A complete A–Z of practical information starts on p.100
- Extensive mapping on cover flaps

Berlitz Publishing Company, Inc.

Princeton   Mexico City   Dublin   Eschborn   Singapore

Text: Jack Altman
Editors: Sarah Hudson
Photography: Jon Davison
Cover photo: © Corel Corporation
Layout: Media Content Marketing, Inc.
Cartography: Visual Image

Thanks to the Greek National Tourist Organisation for their valuable assistance in the preparation of this book.

*Found an error we should know about? Our editor would be happy
to hear from you, and a postcard would do. Although we make every
effort to ensure the accuracy of all the information in this book,
changes do occur.*

ISBN 2-8315-6420-4
Revised 1998 – Second Printing December 1998

Printed in Switzerland by Weber SA, Bienne
029/812 RP

CONTENTS

CRETE

Mediterranean, which here separates Crete from North Africa, just 200 km (125 miles) away).

A series of mountain ranges running north to south divides the island into several distinct regions. The central Ida and Lasíthi (or Díkti) ranges contain, respectively, Crete's highest peak, Psilorítis (Mount Ida), at 2,456 metres (8,058 feet), and the legendary birthplace of the god Zeus in a cave atop Mount Díkti. The Ida Mountains open out to the broad, fertile Messará Plain, Crete's most productive agricultural area. The Díkti mountains encircle a high upland plain, the Lasíthi Plateau, where a ring of pastoral villages surrounds neat, abundant orchards and fields dotted with windmills. The harshly beautiful Sitía range cordons off the remote eastern tip of the island.

Most spectacular of all are the Lefká Ori, or White Mountains, to the west. Although they fall just a few feet short of Mount Ida's peak, overall they are Crete's highest range. Craggy and untamed, these dramatic mountains are sliced by deep gorges that extend all the way down to the sea. Their formidable slopes shelter proud, isolated villages with a turbulent past.

The mountains are primarily limestone, and more than 3,000 caves, from very simple grottoes to vast caverns, have been discovered here. Earthquakes are another feature of Crete's geology, owing to its position on the faultline between the Eurasian and African plates. Modern cities as well as the ancient palaces have suffered from these natural disasters.

In ancient times, Crete was covered in thick woodland. Over the centuries, much of the vast cypress forest was hacked down by foreign conquerers as a source of timber for their ships. The rest was destroyed to make room for the olive trees—an estimated 13 million of them—which thrive on even the harshest slopes. Black netting is unfurled beneath the trees at harvest time to catch the olives as they fall. Olives are a staple crop for the islanders, their oil providing a major source of export revenue. The olive harvest and pressing is a communal activity in many villages.

Crete has a typical Mediterranean climate. Summers are long, hot, and dry; winters see variable rainfall, most of which falls in the mountains, which are snowcapped until June. Thus Cretans depend on snow-melt and groundwater to keep the island green.

Despite the lack of reliable rainfall, the island is incredibly lush. Dense strings of palm trees fringe the beaches at Vái

and Préveli. There are orange groves in the west and banana plantations in the east, both producing notably sweet and delicious fruit. In between are bountiful vineyards and gardens, as well as orchards of apricots, figs, almonds, melons, pomegranates, and quinces—a fruit believed to have originated in Crete—most of which can also be found in the wild.

Crete is a true paradise for nature lovers. Botanists have chalked up more than 2,000 plant species, including 20 varieties of orchid.

The blissful, clear sea and white sand are never too far away.

Greeks to be among themselves, where outsiders should make an effort to remain discreet.

Tourism and agriculture are the mainstays of Crete's economy. The island was one of the first to develop as a package holiday destination, and many villagers have migrated to the coast to work in the booming tourist resorts. Approximately a fifth of the islanders live and work in the capital, Iráklion. Crete's other principal cities are Chaniá, Réthimnon, Sitía, and Ierápetra.

Half of the working population is engaged in agriculture. Crete's main exports are olive oil, sultanas, and wine. A fairly recent, if unsightly, addition to the island's agricultural wealth is the plethora of plastic-wrapped hothouses growing winter vegetables in the south. Nevertheless, they are proving highly profitable, as traditional Cretan products compete in a world of Danish féta cheese and Euro-olive oil.

Greece's membership in the European Union and the establishment of NATO and American military bases on Crete have brought directives not always to the liking of the independent Cretans. But EU membership has also brought many benefits to Crete, in the form of funds for sewage treatment plants that keep the beaches clean and clear, and investment in light industry such as bottling plants and engineering works.

There is no heavy industry on the island, and the only pollution comes from traffic in the main cities. Most hotels and many homes make use of solar panels to supply hot water. As tourism begins to level off, Crete is now looking for further sources of economic growth to take it into the 21st century while preserving the natural beauty and culture of the island—and the taste of its Minoan ancestors for the good life.

A BRIEF HISTORY

The first inhabitants of Crete were Neolithic cave dwellers who came from Asia Minor during the seventh millennium B.C. They established farms and pastures on the fertile Messará Plain and enjoyed peace and prosperity in the early days, untroubled by the invasions that swept through mainland Greece. The influx of new settlers with Bronze Age skills around 3000 B.C. then ushered in the Minoan era, the first major civilization to arise on European soil.

The Minoans

The Minoans appear to have been a peaceful people—or at least they feared no enemies—for they built their palaces and towns without fortifications. The first palatial structures at Knossós, Phaistós, and Mália were erected around 2000 b.c., but these were destroyed by an earthquake 300 years later. The Minoans simply built new ones, even bigger and more splendid than before.

In the Beginning

The Levantine and European roots of Cretan culture appear in Greek mythology. A Phoenician princess was gathering flowers near the shore when she noticed a handsome, pure-white bull grazing nearby. Playful rather than fierce, it let her ride on its back and garland its horns. Suddenly it carried her out to sea and swam to the island of Crete. There, the bull turned out to be Zeus in disguise. He ravished the princess under a plane tree in Górtis. Their union produced Minos, king of Knossós, and his two brothers. The princess's name: Europa.

The designs were purely for pleasure: decorative entrances, roof terraces facing the beautiful countryside, elaborately frescoed bedrooms, and some relatively sophisticated plumbing for the bathrooms. But the rooms themselves, and the small sanctuaries and chapels in which the Minoans worshipped their female deities, were intimate and very much on a human scale. Images of the Mother Goddess were finely sculpted as small figurines rather than imposing statues. Rites of purification and rituals designed to harness divine power, symbolized by the bull, were central to their religion.

The Minoans were ruled by a priest-king, who presided over both religious and economic affairs. It is unclear whether he reigned over the entire island, or if each palace settlement had its own regional king. Women enjoyed high status and played an active part in palace life. According to scenes depicted in the palace frescoes, the Minoans were a handsome, playful people who loved athletic contests and games. Above all, they excelled in the visual arts. At its height, the population of Minoan Crete probably numbered more than 2 million, about four times greater than today's figure, with 100,000 in Knossós alone.

Giant pithoi held olive oil, wine and grain.

The Minoans were one of the great naval powers of the Mediterranean, with the wood from the vast cypress forests providing material for boats. But they concentrated their power more on the commercial than the military, serving a taste for the good life rather than any hunger for an empire.

The fertile land produced enough wine, olive oil, and honey for export. Copper and tin were imported for bronze and refashioned by skilled Minoan artists. Cretans carried on a brisk trade with the Middle East and Egypt, as well as with the other Greek islands. They bought lapis lazuli from Afghanistan, ivory from Syria, and gold, silver, and black obsidian from Anatolia to make their elegant jewellery.

But this great civilization came to a sudden, catastrophic end around 1450 B.C. The exact cause remains unknown, but all the palaces were destroyed at the same time; charred remains at Knossós and volcanic ash at Zákros suggest a great

Family Affairs

Crete's Minoan civilization was named after the mythical King Minos of Knossós. In order to secure his claim to the throne, Minos asked Poseidon to send him a white bull from the sea. But when the beautiful animal emerged, Minos reneged on his promise to sacrifice it to the god. So Poseidon inflamed Minos's wife Pasiphae with passion for the bull, and the offspring of this torrid union was the Minotaur.

Minos hid the bull-headed monster with a human body in a labyrinth. Every nine years, the king fed him 14 youths from Athens. The Athenian hero Theseus vowed to end the slaughter. He seduced the king's daughter Ariadne, who gave him a ball of thread so that he could find his way out of the labyrinth after killing the Minotaur. Theseus escaped from Crete with Ariadne, only to abandon her on a beach in Naxos. Heroes are not always gentlemen.

conflagration. The leading theory is that natural disaster struck the island in the wake of the volcanic explosion on the island of Thíra (Santorini), due north of Crete, bringing a maelstrom of tidal waves, earthquakes, and fire storms. But other scholars believe that an attack by invaders or rebel forces may have brought about the end of this fine culture.

Dorians and Romans

After the disaster, Mycenean Greeks from the Peloponnese moved in to control what remained of the Minoan cities. Around 1200 B.C., Dorian invaders from the Balkans drove south through the Greek mainland and across to Crete.

Many coastal dwellers migrated to remote mountain villages in order to escape their enemies. Others embarked on an overseas exodus that took them as far as Palestine, where the Israelites referred to them as Philistines. The island did

Step back into ancient times when you visit an ancient Minoan ruin.

not get involved in Greece's Persian and Peloponnesian Wars, but it became known as a valuable source of brave and energetic mercenaries.

While mainland Greece was reaching its golden height during the Classical Age (480–338 B.C.), the island remained a backwater of warring city-states, of which Górtis was the most powerful. Nevertheless, the enlightened Athenians acknowledged Crete as a source of much of their culture, and its caves and shrines were major centres of pilgrimage. The island's most important achievement—and only significant remnant—from this period is the law code of Górtis (see page 45). It reveals a hierarchical society of free men, serfs, and slaves, ruled by an aristocratic class.

It took the Romans three years of brutal fighting to conquer Crete in 67 B.C., and even then they did so only by playing off the rival city-states against one another. Crete

The Cretan Renaissance

After the fall of Constantinople in 1453, Crete became a haven for artists and theologians fleeing the Turks. A religious college for the study of painting, theology, and the humanities was established at Iráklion's Church of St. Catherine and it became the centre of the Cretan Renaissance during the 16th and 17th centuries. El Greco is said to have studied here, along with his contemporary, Michaïl Damaskinós, and Vicénzos Kornáros, author of the epic poem *Erotókritos*.

The Cretan artists excelled at icon painting, blending traditional Byzantine style with Venetian influences of Renaissance Italy. Their work was in demand throughout the Western world. Damaskinós, who worked in Venice from 1577 to 1582, was the master of this art. His use of colour and perspective brought a depth to the icon tradition that was widely imitated.

remained a province of the Roman Empire until A.D. 395, with Górtis as its capital.

The Romans managed to bring a certain order to the island, putting an end to internal struggles, building new roads, ports, and aqueducts, and introducing systems of domestic plumbing and central heating not greatly inferior to those found today.

Christian Birthpains

The apostle Paul arrived in A.D. 59 with his disciple Titus, whom he left behind to convert the islanders to Christianity. Titus had a hard time combatting the Cretans' pagan beliefs, and was martyred for his overzealous efforts. But Christianity triumphed, to achieve the strong Orthodoxy of today.

When Roman power split in two, the Byzantine Empire inherited the island. Cretans then remained loyal to the Orthodox Church throughout later Arab occupation (A.D. 824–961).

The Arabs systematically destroyed the churches, turning the island into a pirate base and one of the Mediterranean's principal slave markets. Their fortified capital lay at Rabdh-al-Khandak (Iráklion). When he eventually recaptured the island, however, the Byzan-

The beautiful Saint Vierge at the Toploú Monastery.

tine commander, Nikephóros Phokás, was no more tender-hearted. In order to impress the Arabs holding out in the fort, he catapulted Moslem prisoners' heads over the wall.

Venetian Days

After Byzantium fell to the Crusaders, Crete was given to Boniface of Montferrat, who sold it for cash (1,000 silver marks) to Venice. Crete prospered greatly under the 465 years of Venetian occupation (1204–1669). As a source of ship-building timber in a key location, the island was a king-pin in the farflung commercial empire, and became the Republic's first formally constituted overseas colony.

Proudly emblazoned with the Lion of St. Mark, the ports and fortifications of Chaniá, Réthimnon, and Iráklion bear witness to the Venetians' ambitious public building pro-gramme. Several handsome villas and loggias also attest to their gracious style of living. Typically, the Cretans at first resisted the new foreign rulers with bloody revolts, but grad-

Copies of the Phaistós Disk, unearthed at Phaistós Palace, are reproduced and sold in a myriad of forms as souvenirs.

ually settled down to intermarry with the occupiers and even participate in their style of government.

The arts flourished during the 16th and 17th centuries, a period known as the Cretan Renaissance. The great literary figure of the time, Vitsénzos Kornáros, wrote a romantic epic poem in the Cretan dialect, *Erotókritos*. Even if it has since lost its traditional hold in the mountain villages, it is still declaimed among the literati of Réthimnon.

The Battle for Crete

The Turks waged a titanic struggle to wrest Crete from the Venetians. It began with raids on Chaniá and Sitía in the 1530s by the notorious pirate, Barbarossa Khair el-Din, sailing from Algeria.

Over the next century, the Venetians greatly strengthened the fortifications of what they saw as the last Christian bastion against Turkey's advance in the western Mediterranean. But Chaniá and Réthimnon fell in 1645.

Two years later, the Turks laid siege to the capital, Candia (Iráklion), whose 12,000 civilians were already beset by the plague. The siege was to last 22 years. After the first 15 years, the Turkish commander, Hussein Pasha, was summoned back to Constantinople and publicly strangled for his failure to take the city.

In spite of their Christian allies' perennial reluctance to send adequate support (most notably the bombastic effort of Louis XIV's troops a year before the end), the Venetians' resistance was prodigious. The city's capture in 1669 resulted in the deaths of 30,000 Venetians and 118,000 Turks. As the conquerors entered by the city gates, the Venetians made a negotiated orderly departure, taking with them the cherished head of Saint Titus. This relic of the island's patron saint was only returned in 1966.

Turkish Rule

Crete's years spent under the Turks (1669–1898) constituted a period of cultural and economic stagnation. After the occasionally oppressive, but often brilliant, centuries of Venetian government, Crete slid back into the dark ages.

The rule of the pashas was both exacting and indolent—they built no new mosques, preferring to convert existing churches, and left only a few houses and ornate street fountains as vestiges of their presence. During this time, many Cretans nominally converted to Islam to escape heavy taxes, but continued to practise their Orthodox faith in secret.

The darkness was broken by outbursts of revolt launched from mountain strongholds—for which communities on the plains paid a high price in the form of bloody reprisals. The first major rebellion occurred in 1770 when the Russians, hoping to distract the Turks while they waged their own attacks on the Ottoman Empire elsewhere, promised support to Dhaskaloyiánnis, a wealthy ship-owner. He raised a revolt in Sfakiá, but support never arrived. The rebellion was crushed, Dhaskaloyiánnis was executed, and the event became the subject of a rousing epic poem. Once Greece had achieved independence from the Ottoman Empire after the war of 1821, Crete had to endure nearly a century more of subjection to Turkish oppression and the whims of the Great Powers.

The ferocity of the Cretan combat against the Turks, proclaiming "freedom or death," had all the trademarks of their fiercely independent spirit. Violent insurrections provoked equally violent massacres in retaliation; and death came to form a collective badge of honour of epic proportions.

The island's repeated suffering was duly celebrated in the popular heroic *Songs of Dighenis* (adapted from their medieval origins for the modern struggle), Pandelis Prevelakis' grim novel, *The Cretan*, and the lofty writings of Níkos Kazantzákis.

Union with Greece

Finally, in 1898, the European powers forced the Turks to grant Crete autonomy within the Ottoman Empire and accept Prince George, second son of the Greek king, as governor. However, the prince was forced to resign only a few years later under threat of revolt and the demand for union with Greece. It was only in 1913, under the leadership of Elefthérios Venizélos, a native Cretan, that the longed-for *énosis* (union) was achieved.

Though unscathed by World War I, Crete felt the strain of the forced population exchange between Greece and Turkey in 1923. Thousands of Turks were evacuated, and thousands more Greek refugees from Asia Minor arrived to take their place. Over the years, agricultural resources were improved, and excavations of Minoan palaces brought a new prosperity, as the 20th-century phenomenon of tourism grew.

War and Peace

Crete's pains were not yet over. During World War II, the rapid advance of the German forces through Greece in 1941 forced the Allies to retreat to Crete. On 20 May, German troops invaded the island and secured the airfield to the west of Chaniá. British, Australian, and New Zealand soldiers joined Cretan militia during a valiant defence in the ten-day Battle of Crete, but were ultimately forced to retreat across the island. Many were evacuated to Egypt, though several thousand were left stranded and fled to the mountains. Casualties on both sides were terrible: Allied losses numbered 2,000 killed and 12,000 taken prisoner, while the German war cemetery at Máleme contains almost 4,500 graves.

With their tradition of resistance to foreign invaders, Cretans kept up constant guerrilla warfare against the occupying force. Efforts to shelter the Allies and smuggle them off the island in small groups from isolated south, coast beaches were remarkably successful. But the German army wreaked brutal reprisals on the civilians. In 1944 the resistance pulled off an amazing coup by kidnapping the German commander, General Kreipe, and smuggling him off the island. German troops later marched through the Amári Valley, burning villages to the ground and killing any men they could find. The occupation of Crete did not end until May 1945.

Much of the island was left in ruins from heavy bombing, and some places succumbed to the hasty postwar building boom. But Crete escaped the internal strife of the civil war that raged in mainland Greece (1947–1949). Greece's economic prospects have strengthened since it joined the European Union in 1981. Crete in particular has been a beneficiary of the increase in tourism, to become one of the most prosperous regions of the country.

The imposing parapets of Réthimnon's Venetian fortress.

HISTORICAL LANDMARKS

7000-3000 B.C. Neolithic settlers arrive from Asia Minor.

3000 Bronze Age culture develops on Crete.

2000-1700 Early Palatial Period. First Minoan palaces are built but later destroyed by earthquakes.

1700-1450 Neopalatial Period. Many grand new palaces are built. Most Minoan remains date from this period.

1450 And unknown disaster destroys Minoan civilization.

1400-1100 Post-Palatial Period. Mycenean troops establish settlements at Knossós and Archanes.

1100-67 Dorians overrun Crete, and the rival city-states emerge.

67 Romans conquer Crete and build their capital at Górtis.

A.D. 59 St. Paul and St. Titus bring Christianity to the island.

395 Crete becomes part of the Byzantine Empire.

824-961 Arab occupation of Crete.

961-1204 Liberation of Crete and the Second Byzantine period.

1204-1669 Venetian Period. Fortresses constructed at Iráklion, Chaniá, Réthimnon and Sitía.

1453 Fall of Constantinople. Renaissance of Byzantine art on Crete.

1669-1898 Turkish occupation of Crete.

1898 Crete gains autonomy under Prince George.

1913 *Énosis* (union) with Greece.

1941 German invasion at the Battle of Crete.

1947-49 Greek Civil War.

1951 Greece becomes a member of NATO.

1967-74 Military junta rules Greece.

1972 Iráklion becomes capital of Crete.

1981 Greece joins European Community (EU).

WHERE TO GO

There is so much to explore that it would be impossible to cover all of the island's attractions in a visit of one or two weeks. However, with a little planning you can get a flavour of what Crete has to offer. Mornings are best for visiting the ancient ruins, Byzantine churches, and Venetian monuments, before the heat of the day sets in. Then spend the afternoon on a scenic drive along the coast or into the cool mountain interior, or simply soaking up the sun and sea. When visiting churches and monasteries, bear in mind that Crete tends towards the conservative regarding attire. Lest you forget, prominent signs outside the doors will proclaim "No shorts!"

First-time visitors will want to see Knossós and the other major archaeological sites that are found in central and eastern Crete. Apart from the atmospheric towns of Chaniá and Réthimnon, the attractions of western Crete lie in its stunning mountain excursions. The larger, livelier resorts are located along the northeast and northwest coasts, while the south coast is quieter and, as yet, less developed.

No matter where you are based, try to see some of the surrounding region, which can often be surprisingly different inland. Bus connections are good between the main towns, but it's best to hire a car so that you can explore the mountain villages at your leisure. Note that while distances may seem small on a map, the sharply curving roads and steep gradients can add considerably to your driving time.

Sites of interest on the south shores are divided by rugged mountains and there are no through-roads along the coast. Thus we have included them in respective sections on central, eastern, and western Crete.

IRÁKLION

The Cretan capital of Iráklion, with its busy airport only 4 km (2½ miles) from the city and its ever bustling freight and ferry docks, is the centre of commerce and industry as well as the main gateway for visitors. It ranks fifth in size among Greek cities, but first in terms of income per capita—a surprising fact, as there are few signs of wealth in this untidy sprawl of urbanity. Though it is undeniably noisy, crowded, grimy, and restless, Iráklion nonetheless warrants a visit for a day or two, for its beautiful Venetian fortress, its access to Knossós, and, above all, its Archaeological Museum, one of the best in Greece, with an unsurpassed collection of Minoan treasures. A good way to enjoy the city's attractions is to make excursions *into* town from a coastal resort.

> **SIGNS:**
> ΑΦΙΞΗ – **arrival**
> ΑΝΑΧΩΡΗΣΗ – **departure**

Relax on the shore of Lake Voulisméni in Ágios Nickólaos and watch the boats glide by.

The Town

Centuries of earthquakes (the last big one in 1926) and some severe bombardment during World War II destroyed most vestiges of old-town charm and brought a flurry of drab modern concrete structures in their wake. But a few handsome reminders of the Venetian glory days remain.

Iráklion's most impressive monument is the old **Venetian Fortress,** floating grandly out on its jetty beyond the colourful array of yachts, caïques, and fishing boats in the inner harbour. Built between 1523 and 1540, it was the bulwark of resistance to the long Turkish siege in the 17th century. Emblazoned on the great stone walls are three sculptured lions of St. Mark, the Venetian emblem. The finest one faces seaward and can be viewed from a walk out along the mole. You can tour the fort's restored interior chambers and climb up to the ramparts for a view over the harbour.

Farther along on the quay is the ferry port, where ships arrive and depart for Piraeus near Athens and various Greek is-

Finding Your Way

There is no hard and fast rule for the Roman-lettered versions of Greek names on signposts and road maps. Thus you'll see Iráklion and Heraklion, Hersónissos and Chersonísos, and what we call Chaniá may also turn up as Hania, Khania, and even Xania. Ayía and Agía (both pronounced like the "y"in "yes") are also commonly interchanged.

We have used the names most generally accepted, but be prepared for variations. It will be easier to get about if you familiarize yourself with the Greek alphabet (see page 115) and its pronunciation. Street signs are written in capitals. The words for street (odós), avenue (leofóros), and square (platía) are used in speech, but omitted from signs. Two words to note are Áno (upper) and Káto (lower), designating upper and lower parts of a village, e.g., Áno Zákros and Káto Zákros.

*Behind Chaniá's picturesque waterfront
rise the distant forms of the White Mountains.*

lands. Across the street are the old arcades of the **Arsenali**, where ships were repaired and fitted out for battle. From behind the harbour bus station, you can walk around the **Venetian walls** encircling the inner city. The promenade, some 3 km (2 miles) long, and gives views of the town. It runs south past a pleasant park to the **Promachón Martinéngo** (Martinengo Bastion), burial place of Crete's great 20th-century writer Níkos Kazantzákis.

From the fortress, Odós 25 Avgoústou (25 August Street) leads into the town centre. On the left, fronted by a large square, is the **Church of Ágios Títos** (St. Titus). This eclectic building was originally built by the Venetians, then converted into a mosque by the Turks, before finally being reconsecrated for Orthodox worship in 1922. Contemporary renovations gave the church its airy, modern feel, but the Islamic influences are apparent in the sky-blue domes and arches. A reliquary holds the skull of St. Titus, the island's patron saint.

Next door, adjoining the City Hall (*Dimarkheíon*), is the marvellous reconstructed **Venetian Loggia,** built in 1628 and used by noblemen as a kind of gentleman's club. Its porch is now decorated with medallions of famous Cretans. Across the street, shady **Párko El Gréko** (El Greco Park), with its orange trees and children's playground, provides welcome respite on a hot day. A post office substation and the telecommunications office (OTE) are located here. The former cathedral of **Ágios Márkos** (St. Mark) is just across from the lion fountain. This 13th-century Venetian church was also turned into a Turkish mosque, and the spacious interior is now used as a centre for concerts and contemporary art exhibitions.

Platía Venizélou (Venizélos Square) is a hub of activity for both locals and tourists. Surrounded by cafés, it is a popular meeting point and the best place to sample *bougátsa*, the local custard-filled pastry, as you watch the world pass by. The square honours Crete's great statesman, Eleuthérios Venizélos. However, it's better known as "Fountain Square" after its ornate centrepiece, the **Morosini Fountain,** named after the Venetian governor who had it built in 1628. The fierce lions supporting it are 14th-century works, probably from another fountain.

From the square, follow Odós Kalokerinoú towards the three churches on Platía Agías Ekaterínis. The 15th-century **church of Agía Ekateríni** (St. Catherine), once a dependancy of St. Catherine's desert monastery at Mount Sinai, was a centre for arts and learning during Venetian times. It is now a museum of medieval religious art, with icons, frescoes, wood carvings, and other items from Cretan churches. The two-headed eagle you'll notice in many Orthodox artworks was a symbol of the power of the Byzantine empire. The highlight of this museum is the six large icons by Damaskinós (16th century). These master works are on show in the central nave: *Adoration of the Magi*, *The Last Supper*, *The Burning Bush*, *The Divine Liturgy*, *The Ecumenical Consilium,* and *Noli me tangere* (Christ with the Holy Women).

Also on the square are a 19th-century cathedral and a charming little 15th-century church alongside, both dedicated to St. Mínas. The latter has a gilded iconostasis with grapevine and dragon motifs. Iráklion's colourful, bazaar-like **central market** is located on Odós 1866, just off Fountain Square. Stroll past the butchers, fishmongers, and assorted stalls selling fruit and vegetables, herbs and spices, honey, olives, cheeses, and baked goods, to come out at Platía Kornárou. Here an old Turkish fountain has been converted into a shady café. Behind is the **Bembo Fountain** (1588), with a headless Roman statue found at Ierápetra.

From here, it's a short walk up Avérof Óthonos to busy Platía Eleftherías, surrounded by pricy cafés and streams of traffic. Just off the square you'll find the **Archeologikó Mousío** (Archaeological Museum) and, across from it, the **tourist office.** There is an excellent view of the city walls from behind the museum. The pedestrianized shopping street, **Daedálou,** is lined with jewellery and souvenir shops, leads back to Fountain Square.

The regal lions of the Morosoni Fountain keep watch in busy Venizélos Square.

Near the waterfront west of the fortress, the **Historical and Ethnological Museum** is housed in the former home of Mínos Kalokairinós, who discovered the first remains at Knossós in 1878. It has exhibits from the Byzantine, Venetian, and Turkish periods, Crete's War of Independence against the Turks, and the Nazi occupation during World War II. An early painting by El Greco, depicting the St. Catherine Monastery at Mount Sinai, and a reconstruction of author Níkos Kazantzákis's study, are star attractions. Cretan village traditions are illustrated in a collection of folk art, textiles, and costumes on the top floor.

Archaeological Museum

This is the highlight of Iráklion. Its collection of Minoan artefacts is the finest in the world, rivalling the National Museum in Athens as a repository of the ancient world. You will better appreciate the former splendour of Knossós,

The Lily Prince—a priest-like fresco at Knossós.

Phaistós, and other Minoan sites if you first peruse the exquisite pottery, jewellery, frescoes, and artworks excavated from their ruins. Plan to spend several hours here to take it all in, or make a return visit (tickets are valid for re-entry the same day). Get here first thing in the morning if you want to avoid the guided tours.

The 20 galleries progress chronologically from Neolithic to Roman times. Here are the highlights (please note, though, that displays are frequently rearranged, so objects may not appear in the rooms as noted).

Among the earliest finds in **Room 1,** a **clay bull** with acrobats clutching its horns shows the ancient origins of the bull sports that were later so central to palace life; also on display are early examples of **Vasilikí ware** pottery (see page 37).

In **Room 2,** from the early Palatial Period (2000-1700 B.C.), the **town mosaics** are earthenware plaques from Knossós showing models of the flat-roofed, multi-storeyed Minoan houses. These would have been typical in towns such as Gourniá (see page 58). The first **Kamáres ware** pottery (see page 37) is significant.

The **Phaistós Disk** on display in **Room 3** also comes from the early Palatial Period. Though the hieroglyphic inscription spiralling to the centre of this 16 cm (6 inch) clay disk remains undeciphered, the tiny figures of animals, birds, insects, and people are delightful. What may have been a religious hymn or a magical incantation is now reproduced in the island's souvenir shops as earrings, key chains, and even cocktail coasters.

The Name Game

It is thought that Iráklion began as a Minoan seaport. It functioned as the port, Knossós well into Roman times, when it was known as Herakleium (after Hercules' Seventh Labour). The ninth-century Arab conquerors dug a moat around the city and called it Rabdh-al-Khandak (castle of the moat). The Venetian rulers gave both the island and its capital its medieval name of Candia. During Turkish times, Cretans called the city Megalo Kastro (great fortress), and elderly residents still refer to it this way. Iráklion's present appellation was officially adopted in 1922.

Room 4 abounds with treasures from the golden Neopalatial age (1700–1450 B.C.). Two faïence **snake goddesses** from Knossós, bare-breasted with snakes coiling round the waist, head, and arms, may be priestesses engaged in sacred ritual. Adjacent is a beautiful ivory **gaming board** decorated in blue faïence, crystal, and gold leaf. The striking **Bull's Head Rhyton** (chalice), carved from black steatite with inlaid eyes, was used for ceremonial libations. Along with an alabaster head of a lioness (another rhyton), a panther-head sceptre from Mália, and an ivory bull-leaping acrobat in full flight, it shows the naturalistic skill of Minoan craftsmen. Also impressive is a giant bronze ceremonial sword from Mália.

Room 5 displays tablets of Linear A (the mysterious, and as yet undeciphered, early Minoan script) and Linear B (a later script with mainland Greek influences), plus an explanation of the Linear B accounting system. **Room 6** has a superb boar's tusk helmet.

Three great **bronze double axes** tower on wooden poles near the entrance to **Room 7.** Among the jewellery here is the gold **honeybee pendant** from a tomb near Mália showing two bees joined around a honeycomb. This room also has three Neopalatial stone vases from Agía Triáda, remarkable for their vivid carving. The **Harvester Vase** is

the liveliest, showing peasants laughing and singing behind a priest and musicians in an autumn procession. The other two show a chieftain receiving a gift

Minoan women captured in a fresco at Knossós.

of animal hides from a hunt, and boxing and wrestling matches in progress.

Room 8 contains a fabulous **rock crystal rhyton** with a beaded handle from the palace at Zákros. It was discovered in more than 300 fragments and was painstakingly reconstructed by the museum. Also note the **peak sanctuary rhyton** decorated with wild goats and birds, an important find that revealed several aspects of Minoan worship.

You will notice **seal stones** throughout the museum, but the largest collection is in **Room 9.** Intricately carved on hard stones, they portray all aspects of Minoan life, from nature scenes to religious rituals. They were used to fasten parcels and sign correspondence; those made of precious stones were possibly amulets.

Upstairs in **Room 14,** the **Hall of Frescoes** displays the frescoes of Knossós in all their glory. The recreation of full artworks from the few original fragments that survived seems as

Minoan Art

Minoan art is characterized by movement, light, and colour. This is most evident in the palace frescoes, which depict humans, animals, and plants with a humour and sensuality more akin to ancient Egypt than to the later formal art of Classical Greece. The Minoans followed the Egyptian practice of painting men's skin red, women's white; silver is represented as blue, gold as yellow, and bronze as red. The vibrant colours were created from plant dyes, minerals, and shellfish.

Minoan pottery was graceful and decorative right from the start. Early potters produced the mottled effect by uneven firing seen in Vasilikí ware. Kamáres ware sported red, white, and blue designs on dark backgrounds. The finest pieces, from Phaistós, show floral motifs. Marine motifs and nature themes, painted in dark colours on a light base, emerged later.

amazing a feat as that portrayed in the well-known *Bull Leaping Fresco*. The priest-king, or *Lily Prince*, and the *Dolphin Fresco* are both here, together with the magnificent **Sarcophagus of Agía Triáda,** 3,000 years old, cut from a single block of limestone. One side shows an animal sacrifice, the other scenes of a funeral procession and a bloodless sacrifice for the dead. Also in this room is a wooden **model** of the Knossós palace, which will help you get an idea of its labyrinthine layers.

Rooms 15 and **16** contain more frescoes, most notably the lovely priestess nicknamed *La Parisienne*, and the *Saffron Gatherer*, originally believed to be a boy picking crocuses but later reconstructed as the *Blue Monkey*.

Nearby Beaches

The nearest beach lies to the east beyond the airport, accessible by public bus. Along this stretch there's a municipal beach (you pay a fee) and two others farther along at **Amnísos** and **Tobrúk.** However, be prepared to put up with the constant noise of incoming planes.

A better bet is the broad, sandy beach that lies some 6 km (4 miles) to the west of Iráklion at **Amoudára** and, farther along, **Linoperámata.** The beach is pleasant, despite the incongruous smokestacks of the power station puffing away at the western end.

CENTRAL CRETE

The major archaeological sites of Knossós, Górtis, Phaistós, and Agía Triáda lie south of Iráklion, following the path of the old Minoan road through the valleys between the Ida and Lasíthi mountains to the south coast. Knossós needs a day to itself. The others can be visited in a single day trip (though be sure to get an early start) either by rental car or on a guided tour.

Knossós

This the largest of the **Minoan palaces,** lies just 5 km (3 miles) south of Iráklion; it is easily reached by public bus from the city (leaves from Odos Evans, near the market). Neolithic remains have been discovered beneath the central court and, subsequent to the fall of the Minoan reign, Knossós remained an important town for later settlers well into Roman times.

The first palace was built just after 2000 B.C., but was destroyed by an earthquake 300 years later. It was promptly rebuilt in even greater splendour, and the remains you see

Partly reconstructed, the palace of King Minos still evokes the splendour of his ancient court.

today are from this Neopalatial period. At its peak the palace had approximately 1,200 rooms on five levels, and was surrounded by a sizeable town. Then, around 1450 B.C., the great civilization that flourished here was wiped out in an unknown catastrophe (see page 18).

Knossós lay buried until Mínos Kalokairinós, a Cretan archaeologist, uncovered the storerooms in 1878. The find attracted the attention of Heinrich Schliemann, the obsessive German excavator of Troy and Mycenae, but he was unable to acquire the site. Some 16 years later the Englishman Arthur Evans, then director of Oxford's Ashmolean Museum, began scratching around after clay tablets and seal stones.

Evans was a wealthy man and a visionary. Intrigued by Knossós, he bought the land and began digging in earnest in 1900. Within two years, most of the palace area was exposed —rather too quickly, in fact, as much information was lost or badly documented. In order to preserve and understand the complexity of the various levels, Evans reconstructed parts of the palace as he thought they must have looked in Minoan times, making use of available evidence and incorporating some of the original fragments into the pillars and supports of reinforced concrete. His romantic restoration has often been criticized by later archaeologists. Still, his colourful presentation enables visitors to visualize, something of the awesome grandeur of the Minoan world at its height.

Many identify the palace of Knossós with the labyrinth of the mythical King Minos (see page 18), and there may be some etymological basis for the belief. The pre-Hellenic word *labrys*, meaning "double axe," coupled with the ending *nthos*, gives the meaning "house of the double axe"; one of the characteristic finds at Knossós is indeed the double axe.

Whether or not Knossós is the literal labyrinth of the legend, the sprawling complex is certainly maze-like, with its connecting rooms, narrow passages, raised walkways, odd landings, and L-shaped stairways leading up and down and in and out of courtyards and vestibules. Don't worry if you lose your way, even with a map. The home of Minos invites wandering, and eventually you will come across the major points of interest.

You enter Knossós through the **west court,** past the bronze bust of Sir Arthur Evans. The circular walled pits were used as repositories for devotional offerings at the end of sacred rituals. Note the stone blocks on the western façade, blackened by fire during the destruction of circa 1450 B.C .

Turning right, follow along the **corridor of processions** adorned with frescoes of men and women bearing gifts and ceremonial vessels. All of the frescoes on the site are reproductions (the originals are preserved in the Archaeological Museum in Iráklion).

Ancient Rites

The bull was a symbol of virility to the ancient Minoans, representing the uncontrollable forces of nature. The walls of Knossós were adorned with giant horns of consecration, and spectacular bull-leaping ceremonies in which young acrobats grasped the horns and somersaulted over the back of a charging animal were performed in the central courtyard. In annual rites of renewal, a bull was netted and bound, its throat cut, and its blood drained into sacred vessels. This sacrifice honoured the life force of the bull, connecting the society to its divine power and the growing cycles of the earth.

The Mother Goddess was central to the cult, personified in the breasts (symbols of fertility) of the snake goddess. The snake, shedding its skin, signified reincarnation and healing.

The sacred pillar was a symbol of the goddess, as was the double axe, thought to represent the waxing and waning of the moon. The axe also signified the two-edged power of the priest-king: religious and political.

The way turns left (east) towards the columned vestibule of the **south propylaea.** Notice the characteristic downward taper of the reconstructed columns. The huge horns of consecration mark the location where the original fragments were found. Nearby, the famous **priest-king fresco** commands a view over the palace from an upper chamber.

A staircase leads north up to the **piano nobile.** Evans gave the rooms and frescoes their fanciful names, this one borrowed from the Italian Renaissance. From this upper storey you can look down over the central court and, to the west, over the storerooms with their enormous *píthoi* (storage jars). Ahead are the shrine rooms of the **sanctuary hall**.

Below, off the northwestern corner of the court, stands the **throne room,** with its frescoes of princely griffins. The well-worn gypsum throne is the oldest in Europe. The sunken basin in front was used for purification rites. Few visitors can resist having their photo taken on the wooden replica of the throne in the antechamber. On the other side of the sanctuary's staircase is a columned **crypt** and **treasury,** where cult objects were found, including the snake goddess statues now in the Archaeological Museum. The sacred snakes probably had their homes here.

These Corinthian reminders lie scattered among the ruins at Górtis, the Roman capital built in 67 B.C.

The **central court,** approximately 55 metres (180 feet) long and 28 metres (92 feet) wide, lies at the heart of the palace. In Minoan times it would have been surrounded by high walls. This is where the athletic contests and great bull-leaping rituals so vividly depicted in the frescoes and sculptures were held.

On the east side of the court, the **grand staircase** descends to what Evans identified as the **royal chambers.** These are the best preserved rooms. Set into the slope of the hill, the quarters were built on four levels. Lighting was channelled down to rooms on lower floors through an ingenious system of spacious light wells.

Shields and signs of the double axe mark the walls of what was probably the guardroom to the **king's chamber,** where Evans found a wooden throne. A thin passage leads over to the **queen's chamber,** decorated by a fresco of dolphins and flying fish. Next to it is a room housing a clay bathtub and toilet, with a still-visible flushing system.

The drainage system of terracotta pipes that ran below the palace is much admired, incorporating a means to break and control the flow of water that was amazing for its time. Parts are visible under grilles and at the fringes of this area.

The fresco of playful and colourful dolphins that decorate the queen's chamber are a palace favorite.

North of the royal quarters are the **storehouses** and **workshops** of the palace's tailors, goldsmiths, potters, and stonemasons. In particular, notice the giant *píthoi* used for storing grain, oil, and wine.

Northwest of the palace is a **theatre** seating some 500 spectators. Leading away from it is the **royal road,** thought to be the oldest in Europe. The paving stones are original and date from the third millennium B.C. Once lined with houses and shrines, the road may have run all the way north to the sea.

The Messará Plain

Three of Crete's major archaeological sites lie in the Messará Plain. This is the island's largest agricultural area, its fertile fields covered in olive trees, fruits, and vegetable crops, and wild flowers in the spring.

Take the main road south from Iráklion towards Míres. At **Agía Varvára**, a detour to the west along a dramatic sec-

The ruins of Phaistós command a sweeping view over the green fertile Messará Plain.

ondary road provides beautiful views over the plain and the distant mountains. The road follows the southern flank of Mount Ida towards Kamáres and beyond, where it meets up with the Amári Valley (see page 68). The attractive village of **Zarós** makes a good base for mountain rambles and a splendid walk through the Rouvas Gorge. There are also ancient churches to visit, including **Moní Varsamónero,** with its superb frescoes, and **Moní Vrondísi**, which once housed the Damaskinós icons (now in St. Catherine's in Iráklion).

Back on the main road: the plain opens up after the Pass of Vourvoulítis, 600 metres (2,000 feet) above sea level. The village of **Agii Déka** is named after the ten saints who were martyred here in A.D. 250. There is a Byzantine church at the end of the village, constructed partly from the Roman ruins of Górtis, and a modern chapel nearby with a crypt supposedly containing the martyrs' tombs.

Górtis

Ancient Górtis, the Roman capital founded here in 67 B.C., was a thriving city, numbering up to 300,000 people at its height. Its remains are scattered over a large area, and the best way to enjoy the site is to wander through the fields of olive trees on the south side of the road, discovering for yourself the fascinating remnants of ancient buildings, columns, and capitals.

Fenced in on the north side is Górtis's major attraction. Around 500 B.C., the Dorian settlers carved Europe's first ever **Code of Laws** onto massive stone blocks, now incorporated in a wall of the Roman *odeon*. The 600 rows of archaic Greek script read alternately from left to right and right to left, a style properly known as *boustrophedon*—the so-called ox-plough manner. The code lays down numerous rulings on marriage, divorce, adultery, rape, property, and inheritance rights, and the fines for offences, which differed greatly between freemen and slaves. Many historians regard the code as a vital step in the transition to modern law.

The barrel-vaulted shell of the enormous sixth-century basilica of **Ágios Títos** is the best-preserved Early Christian church on Crete. It was said to be the final resting place of Titus, first bishop of Crete and the island's patron saint. It was destroyed by Arab invaders in A.D. 825.

Phaistós

Of all the ancient sites on the island, Phaistós, the second largest Minoan palace, enjoys the most magnificent setting. Perched on an acropolis some 60 metres (200 feet) above the Messará Plain, it commands a fine panoramic view that includes Mount Díkti to the east, Mount Ida to the north, and the Asteroússia range along the south coast. Henry Miller, visiting shortly before World War II, wrote, "Stone and sky, they marry here."

The palace is said to have been the legendary home of King Minos's brother Rhadamanthys, and like Knossós its rooms and corridors were built around a central courtyard. While no frescoes were found here, the workmanship and materials of marble, alabaster, and gypsum suggest the greatest luxury. Phaistós was actually the site of two successive palaces, constructed and destroyed at the same time as those at Knossós, and remains from both periods are on view. This, coupled with a lack of signage and the presence of ongoing archaeological excavations, make the site somewhat confusing.

Start from a stairway going down from the **north court,** passing on your right (outside the palace grounds), a **theatre** with an elongated shape, like a grand piano. This has a rightful claim as the world's most ancient theatre.

A grander staircase leads left up to the **propylaeum,** the monumental entrance to the palace itself. Left again, across a hall where you can make out the bases of its peristyle colonnade, are the **royal chambers.** East from here are the commoners' dwellings where the Phaistós Disk was dicovered (see page 35).

From the queen's rooms, a small courtyard and corridor lead back south to the long **central court.** Most of the eastern part of the court has collapsed down the hillside, but the column bases of the western portico are all still visible. Walk to the far end to see the palace's principal **well** and then double back past what was the **sanctuary,** where you will see a two-pillared crypt and a hall with stone benches around its walls. Beyond the sanctuary, turn left down the corridor of **storehouses** and **workshops** used for metal smelting and pottery. The last house on the right has some of the huge earthenware storage jars (*píthoi*) used for oil and wine. Notice the many handles through which ropes were passed to haul the gigantic vessels around. At Vóri, just to the north of Phaistós, the **Museum of Cretan Ethnology** shows traditional implements and baskets in an old Cretan house.

Agía Triáda

This Minoan **Royal Villa** is 3 km (2 miles) from Phaistós. As its Minoan name remains a mystery, it's named after a Venetian church (Holy Trinity) southwest of the site (not to be confused with the Byzantine church above the excavations).

Scholars argue over whether the site was a residence of the king's relatives, a ritual centre, a prince's realm, or a summer (more likely winter) retreat for the king himself. With a splendid view out over the Messará Bay (in Minoan times the sea was much closer to the villa), it is spacious but more intimate in its proportions than the palaces, and without a central court. Fine alabaster paving and some treasures unearthed here hint at a former elegance.

North of the Minoan villa is a staircase leading beyond a portico of five pillars to the remains of a later, Dorian town (14th–12th centuries B.C.).

The Beaches

After a hot day of touring ancient sites, you might want to relax on a nearby beach. The small but lively resort of **Mátala** is just 10 km (6 miles) south of Phaistós. The long, curving beach of fine white sand offers excellent swimming in a gentle sea, with colourful fish and the underwater remains of a Roman port as added entertainment for snorkellers.

A string of pleasant tavernas overlooks the beach at one end. At the other are the famous Mátala **caves,** which are hewn out of the sandstone cliffs by the Romans and early Christians for use as catacombs. Over the centuries they were inhabited by local people and used as artillery positions during World War II, finally becoming havens for the hippie troglodytes of the 1960s. The caves are now cleared by the police each night, but during the day you can climb up for a look and a sunny perch above the crowded waterfront. Another, more remote beach, about 2 km (1

The church of Ágia Triáda is thought to have been a summer retreat.

mile) to the east of Mátala, is reached only by a steep path (well-marked).

Farther west, **Agía Galíni** is one of the most picturesque resorts on the island, situated in a crevice between high cliffs. Though booming in summer, it is an off-season delight, its narrow, traffic-free lanes, shaded with cascading bunches of bougainvillaea and jasmine, climbing up from a small harbour. The atmosphere is

> **SIGNS:**
> ΙΛΙΩΤΙΚΗ ΠΛΑΖ
> **– private beach**
> ΑΠΑΓΟΡΕΥΕΤΑΙ
> Η ΚΟΛΥΜΠΗΣΗ
> **– no swimming**

friendly, there are good restaurants, and though the rather small beach has more rocks than sand, it is lined with tavernas.

Mount Ida and the Idaean Cave

Mount Ida, known to the Cretans as **Psilorítis,** "the high one," is Crete's highest summit at 2,456 metres (8,055 feet). Its twin peaks, snowcapped until late spring, are often obscured in a puff of clouds, but on a clear day, when the powerful granite bulk is exposed, you can see why Zeus would have chosen it as his childhood home. The Idéon Ántron (Idaean Cave) was an important pilgrimage centre in ancient times, possibly even the birthplace of the god. You can visit it on a fine drive from Iráklion (but check first with the tourist office, as the cave is sometimes closed). Head west from the city via the old road through Gázi. **Arolíthos,** a purpose-built "traditional" village, is worth a stop to watch its weavers, potters, and icon painters at work.

The route continues through pretty vineyards to **Tílissos.** The ruins of three late, Minoan villas here, in a peaceful spot below towering pines, make a change from the larger sites. As you wander through doorways into small rooms and along walls nearly 2 metres (6 feet) tall, you can imagine what life, here must have been like.

The mountain air of **Anógia** is a refreshing respite from the sweltering lowlands. It is renowned for its fine weaving and embroidery, and for its *lyra* players. The village has a grisly past: it was twice destroyed and rebuilt following rebellions against the Turks in 1821 and 1866; then, in 1944, German troops burnt Anógia to the ground in retaliation for the villagers' part in the abduction of General Kreipe (see page 26). In the square in the upper part of town, a statue of a soldier honours the freedom fighters who were killed in these atrocities. In the lower village, black-clad women sell their textiles while old men in breeches gather at the *kafenía*.

It can take an hour to traverse the 21 km (13 miles) of steep, rough track to the **Nída Plateau.** Along the way are round stone huts once used for making sheep's milk yoghurt and cheese. From the tourist pavilion, a walk leads to the **Idaean Cave.** Legend has it that King Minos came here every nine years to get a new batch of laws from Zeus, making Ida a kind

---

Cretan Caves

Crete's limestone mountains are riddled with caves. More than 3,200 have been recorded, over half the known caves in all of Greece. Many are simple grottoes, others have chambers and passages, with impressive stalactites, stalagmites, and pools of water. Caves figure large in Cretan myths and history. They have been used as dwellings, religious shrines, and refuges in times of trouble. Many are open to visitors (check with the local tourist office for times); take a torch and wear rubber-soled shoes, as floors are often wet and slippery.

Among Crete's most famous caves are the Idaean Cave (see page 49), the Diktaean Cave (see page 56), the Melidóni Cave (see page 67), the Cave of Eileithyia near Iráklion, dedicated to the goddess of childbirth, and the Kamáres Cave on Mount Ida.

of Mount Sinai. Though the cave itself is not impressive, the votive offerings and artefacts dating as far back as 3000 B.C. confirm its importance as an ancient shrine.

Experienced hikers can ascend to the **summit** (7 to 9 hours round trip). Although the route is roughly marked with red dots, a guide is recommended and appropriate gear is essential. At the least wear walking boots and carry spare clothing and plenty of water. There's a chapel at the top for shelter and meditation.

If you're heading west from Anógia, the route through the pleasant towns of **Axós** and **Garázo** offers a look at local village life. Shortly after the junction with the old road to Réthimnon, a detour through the pretty villages of **Agia** and **Melidóni** leads to the spectacular Melidóni Cave (see page 67).

EASTERN CRETE

The north coast east of Iráklion is the most developed part of the island, with sprawling, hedonistic beach resorts within an hour's drive of the airport. Beyond the main resort town of Ágios Nikólaos, the winding corniche road offers stunning views over the coastline all the way to the provincial city of Sitía and beyond.

When you want a rest from the boisterous beach towns, head inland through the mountains to the pastoral charm of the Lasíthi Plateau. There are splendid palace ruins at Mália and Káto Zákros, and a Minoan village at Gourniá. The quieter beaches of the south coast are also easily reached.

Hersónissos and Mália

These popular resorts have mushroomed into brash commercial towns, thanks to a booming package tour trade. A string of hotels, restaurants, nightclubs, souvenir shops, and travel agencies runs for miles along sandy beaches that are among the finest in Crete, though overdevelopment makes this stretch unappealing.

Hersónissos, also spelled Chersónísos or, more correctly, Limín (Port) Hersónissou, has a Roman fountain and a few remnants of its days as an ancient port submerged in the harbour. Otherwise it's dedicated to beach life by day, disco and bar life by night. The same raucous holiday spirit predominates at **Mália,** farther along the coast. On the outskirts, however, you can explore the evocative ruins of a third great **Minoan palace.** With its red-coloured stones warmed by the sun, Mália looks more inviting than many ancient sites. Dating from the same period as Knossós and Phaistós, its features will seem familiar: a large central courtyard with a throne room off the northwest corner, storage chambers with *píthoi* (earthenware jars), lustral basin, and pillar crypt.

Next to the ceremonial staircase off the southwest corner of the court is a remarkable circular **kernós** (ritual table). Set in the limestone slab are 34 depressions around a central hol-

The Birthplace of Zeus

Students of Greek mythology argue over whether the Diktaean Cave or the Idaean Cave on Mount Ida was the birthplace of Zeus. The god's father, Kronos, Lord of the Titans, had devoured his other children because of a prophecy that he would be dethroned by one of his offspring. Zeus's mother Rhea went off to Crete to bear her child in secrecy. The Kouretes beat drums outside the cave to hide his cries. When Kronos came looking for the baby, Rhea fooled him with a stone wrapped in swaddling clothes, which Kronos promptly swallowed.

Thereafter, Zeus grew up secretly in the Diktaean Cave, weaned on goat's milk and Cretan honey. He spent his youth with shepherds on Mount Ida. When he was big enough, he went off and struck down his father with a thunderbolt.

low. One theory is that fruit seeds or grain were placed in the hollows as offerings for a good harvest. It may also have been used as a gaming board.

A short walk north of the palace close to the sea is the **chrysólakkos** (pit of gold), a royal burial chamber where the exquisite gold honeybee pendant now displayed in Iráklion's Archaeological Museum was found (see page 36).

Ágios Nikólaos

The National Highway climbs higher as it cuts inland, making a beeline for Ágios Nikólaos. On the way, you can make a detour to the market town of **Neápolis,** birthplace of Pope Alexander V. There is a folklore museum at the southern end of the main square. Be sure to sample the sweet and cooling local drink, *soumáda*, which is made from pressed almonds.

Ágios Nikólaos, nestled on a hilly peninsula on Mirabéllo Bay, is one of the most popular spots on the island. At its picturesque heart extends **Lake Voulisméni,** fed from an underground river and enclosed on one side by a steep cliff that

Head for the heart of Ágios Nikóloas and Lake Voulisméni.

affords a great view from the top. The freshwater lake, once thought to be bottomless, is in fact 64 metres (210 feet) deep and is connected to the harbour by an artificial channel. You can enjoy the bustling waterfront scene from any one of a number of cafés and restaurants, or join in the evening promenade along the lake's attractive quayside. The **tourist office** is also located here.

Not surprisingly, Ágios Nikólaos is extremely crowded in high season. You can escape on a scenic cruise around pretty Mirabéllo, Crete's largest bay. The tiny, crowded patches of sand that serve as town beaches make for poor swimming, however. Better bets are found farther afield.

The town's **Archaeological Museum** on Odós Paleológou houses an admirable collection of Minoan artefacts from eastern Crete. Its showpiece is the lovely Goddess of Myrtos, actually a whimsical, long-necked jug. Also look out for a rare Minoan burial jar that contains intact the bones of an infant. Equally macabre is a grinning Roman skull with a crown of gold olive leaves. The coin here, once held between its teeth, was to pay the ferryman for the journey across the River Styx to the underworld. For a look at contemporary Cretan art, the **Museum of Popular Art,** located next to the bridge at the beginning of Odós Paleológou, houses popular artcraft of the area.

The mountain village of **Kritsá**, 12 km (7½ miles) inland, is a popular excursion. The town is celebrated for its textiles, and banners of woven rugs and embroidered linens hang from the balconies of the whitewashed houses along the steeply sloping streets.

Slightly below Kritsá, the Byzantine church of **Panagiá Kerá** preserves some of the island's finest frescoes, which date from the 14th and 15th centuries. Those in the south nave depict the early life of Mary and that of her mother

Ann, the central nave has scenes from the life of Christ, while the final aisle portrays the Last Judgement.

Follow the signs leading up to the ruins of **Lató**, a Doric settlement founded in the seventh century B.C., to enjoy its wonderful setting and views overlooking the sea.

Eloúnda and Spinalónga Island

The western shore of Mirabéllo Bay is dotted with several large luxury hotels with private beaches, as well as some smaller places to stay. **Eloúnda,** 12 km (7½ miles) to the north of Ágios Nikólaos, is an increasingly popular resort, more low key and attractive than most others on the north coast. The large square along the harbour is the focal point of town.

Eloúnda's picturesque bay is enclosed by the Spinalónga peninsula (the name means "long thorn" in Italian). Here, near the causeway that joins it to the mainland, the submerged Greco-Roman village of **Oloús** makes a fascinating target for divers. Eloúnda has several good restaurants and a

The island of Spinalónga was made a leper colony in 1903 to encourage Turkish settlers to leave.

beach, though the best beach is farther north at **Plaka,** a tiny fishing village with excellent seafood tavernas.

Harbour cruises from Ágios Nikólaos or Eloúnda take you out to Spinalónga Island, dominated by a 16th-century Venetian fortress. Later Turkish settlers built homes here and refused to leave after Greece won independence. To entice them to go, the government designated the island a leper colony in 1903, disbanded in 1957. You can wander through the eerie ruins of the houses and village, and climb up to the top of the fortress for superb views over the bay.

The Lasíthi Plateau

The Lasíthi Plateau lies high in the Díkti Mountains at some 850 metres (2,800 feet). Its bountiful plains are covered with apple and almond orchards, market gardens, and patchwork fields of potatoes and grains. It is famous for the army of old white cloth-sailed windmills that once drove the irrigation system. Nowadays, the handful that remain have mostly lost their sails and stand as sorry sentries in the fields. Nonetheless, a trip to this idyllic plain is well worth it. The villages here are all charming gems of pastoral life—bearded Orthodox priests chat leisurely with farmers along the roadside, peasant women trot along sidesaddle on donkeys laden with firewood, and archaic tractors potter down the lanes pulling carts heaped with bags of produce.

There are three routes up from Ágios Nikólaos and Iráklion. The most dramatic begins at Neápolis (see page 53), winding up a narrow mountain road past tiny hamlets such as **Zenia** (look out for the craftsman selling wooden spoons along the roadside) and **Exo Potami.** Suddenly the sweeping upland plain opens out before you. A paved road links the towns that encircle the plateau. At the junction, turn left for a visit to the **Diktéon Ántron** (Diktaean Cave), just beyond **Psychró** (Psihro). The cave is a contender for the birthplace of Zeus, and the stone altars and votive offerings that were discovered here point to its role as another important Minoan sanctuary.

Take a warm sweater, non-slip shoes, and a pocket torch to explore the cavern; try to arrive before noon to avoid the crowds. The guides who pester you at the entrance are not essential, but you may find their patter entertaining in pointing out the mythological highlights of the cave.

A steep and tricky passage leads 60 metres (200 feet) down to a cave that is damp, slippery, and dimly lit. The impressive stalagmites and stalactites took on, in the flickering light of pilgrims' lamps, the shape of divinities. One is still known as the Cloak of Zeus.

After your subterranean adventure, head back through **Ágios Geórgios** and pay a brief visit to the **folk museum,** where one room is dedicated to author Níkos Kazantzákis. After **Tzermiádo,** the plateau's largest town, the road climbs to the stunning **mountain pass** at Séli Ambélou. The ruined stone windmills piercing the sky along the top of the ridge were traditional grain mills. There are also dramatic views back over the plain and ahead across the island to the sea, which you are unlikely to forget.

Just on the outskirts of **Kerá**, the convent of **Panagía Kardiótissa** (Our Lady of the Heart) contains several beautiful 14th-century frescoes. At **Krási,** stop for a rest beneath the enormous plane tree, said to be 2,000 years old and the largest in Europe. It takes 12 men to encircle its girth. Sample the local *raki* from the taverna whose outdoor tables surround the tree, and fill up your water bottle from the fountain of the curative spring, said to be good for stomach ailments.

The descent through **Mohós** offers spectacular views over the coast. The village has an attractive square with cafés. The

Swedish prime minister Olof Palme kept a summer house here behind the church, which has become a memorial.

Alternatively, take the route back to the National Highway via **Potamiés** and see the tenthth-century monastery of **Panagía Gouverniótissa** (Assumption of the Virgin), one of the oldest in Crete. A lemon tree graces the peaceful courtyard in front of the chapel, and you can look round the dilapidated dormitory and kitchen ovens.

Gourniá

At about the time Evans began digging at Knossós, Harriet Boyd Hawes, a young American archaeologist, started excavating the ancient Minoan town of Gourniá, some 18 km (11 miles) southeast of Ágios Nikláos. It was well situated on a hillside above a natural harbour at the narrowest point of the island, and connected to the south coast by a carriageway. Although the site was occupied significantly earlier, the remains date from around 1500 B.C.

Here the focus is on everyday life in an ordinary township. The cobbled streets were just wide enough for pack animals, not wheeled transport. The walls of the houses and shops around the marketplace are clearly defined. Tools discovered here identified the homes of various craftsmen. The dwellings seem relatively small, but we know from the town mosaics in the Archaeological Museum that they were multistoried. At the top of the hill are the remains of the governor's palace and its courtyard, as well as a shrine.

Psíra and Móchlos

These two islands on the eastern side of Mirabéllo Bay also have important Minoan settlements, parts of them submerged, offshore. Of the two, tiny **Móchlos** is the easier to visit, just 150 metres (480 feet) out from the very pleasant fishing village that shares its name. If you choose to swim across the channel, remember to take some shoes for clambering over the rough rocks to the ancient houses, chamber-tombs, and Roman fortifications.

Divers exploring the underwater ruins should remember it is a criminal offence to remove any objects. Archaeological finds from here (and from Gourniá) are shared among the museums of Ágios Nikólaos, Sitía, and Iráklion.

Sitía

The heady drive from Ágios Nikólaos to the eastern end of the island affords plunging views over the sea along the corniche road, which is sometimes called the Cretan Riviera. There is a good sandy beach at the scenic cove below **Istro,** but avoid the polluted bay around Pahiá Ammos.

Sitía, Crete's fifth-largest town, has become a laid-back resort, thanks to its port and pleasant waterfront. The area was settled in Minoan times, but earthquakes and Turkish raiders destroyed most visible remains of its subsequent his-

The ruins of Gourniá yield clues to the everyday life in an ancient Minoan town.

tory. The **Venetian fortress,** now used as an open-air theatre in summer, still towers above the town, and there are ruins of Roman fish tanks along the harbour.

The town's **Archaeological Museum** houses regional finds and artefacts from the Minoan palace at Zákros, including a wine press and rare Linear A tablets of the early Minoan script. The town has good beaches and good restaurants. Otherwise, there's little to do but observe everyday life in this enjoyable provincial town, or lounge in the cafés along the harbourfront. Keep an eye out for the town mascot, Níkos the pelican. The locals so enjoyed his antics that they constructed a home for him on the quayside.

East of Sitía, 14th-century **Moní Toploú** (Toploú Monastery) stands in isolated splendour on a windy hilltop; it owns much of the surrounding land and is reputed to be one of the richest monasteries in Greece. Its name means "can-

The Touploú Monastery holds treasured religious masterpieces and memories of wartime.

non" in Turkish, so called after the Venetian artillery installed here to defend it against invaders. It served again as a centre of Cretan resistance in World War II.

You can look inside an old stone windmill to see the massive wooden cylinders used to grind flour. Through the picturesque flowery courtyard, the church and museum hold an important icon by Ioánnis Kornáros entitled *Lord, Thou Art Great* (1770). This masterpiece of Cretan art comprises 60 scenes from the Bible in intricate detail.

Farther to the east, a grove of wild palms suddenly appears like an oasis in the barren countryside. Behind that, the beach at **Váï** attracts innumerable bathers, drawn by the exotic backdrop, fine sand, and translucent green waters. The trees are said to have grown from date stones spat out by Arab invaders. You can also visit a nearby banana plantation; be sure to try some of the Cretan bananas—they're smaller and sweeter than the imported variety.

Káto Zákros

A fourth great Minoan palace lies at the farthest southeastern point of the island. It was originally discovered by a British archaeologist in 1901; the excavation was later financed by an American couple. The road from Sitía curves through the stark, purple-hued landscape of a high plateau in the Sitía mountains before winding down to the sea and a delightful little beach with pleasant tavernas. Most public buses terminate in Áno (upper) Zákros; Káto (lower) Zákros is another 8 km (5 miles) farther on. Alternatively, you can walk to the palace from the upper town through a splendid ravine called the **Valley of the Dead;** the route is marked with red dots and takes approximately two hours.

Linked to its harbour by a stone-paved road, the **Minoan palace** (1600–1450 B.C.) was enriched by the town's flourishing sea trade with Egypt and the Middle East. It was also the island's principal naval base. Because of its isolated position, the palace was forgotten after its destruction. When it was excavated in 1961 by Nikoláos Pláton, it yielded some of the island's best-preserved bronze and stoneware.

Though smaller, Zákros' layout is similar to the other great palaces, with the **shrine** and **ritual bath** to the west and **royal apartments** to the east of the **central court.** The shrine's treasury revealed a magnificent collection of ivory and bronze, with ornate chalices and vases, now on display in the museum at Sitía. The **kitchen** area north of the court came with a nearly complete set of utensils.

Most astonishing of all, in a ritual well-chamber still filled with springwater, was a votive cup of olives, 3,000 years old. Pláton and his team sampled the olives — which began to disintegrate as soon as they were exposed to the air — and found them to be as tasty as if they had just been picked.

Behind the royal apartments is the rectangular **Hall of the Cistern,** with steps leading down to a circular underground pool, unique among the Minoan palaces. It may have been the king's swimming pool, a royal aquarium, or a ceremonial pool for a sacred boat. Climb up to the ancient town area above the palace for a good view over the site.

Ierápetra and the South Coast

The quickest way to the south coast is via the highway, at Pahiá Ammos, that crosses the island at its narrowest point — just 14 km (9 miles) wide. More rewarding, however, is the route south from Sitía, which offers dramatic mountain scenery between the east and west branches of the Sitía range, or the winding road along the edge of the Díkti Mountains from Istro, through **Kalamáfka,** where you can see both coasts simultaneously on a clear day.

Ierápetra is Crete's fourth-largest town, and the southernmost in Europe—Africa is a mere 300 km (187 miles) away. With a Venetian fort, a Turkish mosque, a good beach, and plenty of waterfront tavernas, it is not unattractive, but it often lacks the vitality of other resorts. The fruit market and archaeological museum are minor attractions. In summer, boats go out to **Chrissi Island,** 13 km (8 miles) away, with a cedar forest (the same trees that once covered Crete), pure white sand dunes, and millions of seashells.

To the east of Ierápetra there's a mountainous stretch with a good beach below at **Agía Fotiá.** A little farther on, **Makrigialós** has one of the finest beaches on the south coast, with shallow shelving sand and several pleasant tavernas. New building has joined the village with its neighbour, **Análipsi,** making a relatively low-key, but growing, resort.

In spring and summer, make a visit to the nearby **Dásakis Butterfly Gorge,** a peaceful haven for butterfly species as well as griffon vultures and other birdlife. There is a delightful water garden next to the café. West of Ierápetra, the pretty village of **Myrtos,** climbing up from a stony shore, offers a laid-back escape.

WESTERN CRETE

Apart from Réthimnon and Chaniá, with their atmospheric old Venetian and Turkish quarters and popular resorts, western Crete is quieter than the east, indeed even remote at the far end of the island. It's also lusher and greener than eastern Crete. The magnificent White Mountains, Crete's highest range, offer many exhilarating walks through their gorges, as well as spectacular scenic drives to and from the sleepy fishing ports and smaller beaches of the southwest coast.

Réthimnon's Venetian fortress overlooks the harbour.

☛ Réthimnon

Crete's third, largest city offers the best of both worlds: a fabulous long and sandy beach (which, however, is rapidly being developed with hotels catering to tourists on package tours), and an evocative, historic old quarter to explore. The town is a haven for Cretan artists and writers, and every August a Renaissance festival of music, theatre, and art is held at the old fort.

The awesome 16th-century **Venetian Fortezza** (fortress) towers on the western promontory. It is thought to be the largest Venetian fortress ever constructed. To appreciate its size, walk around the walls along the path above the rocky shoreline, then climb to the top for the fine views over the town and harbour. The interior is like a small city, with chapels, ruined barracks, and arsenals to explore. The huge domed mosque in the centre was converted from a church during the Turkish occupation; inside, the bright tiles of its decorative prayer niche are visible beneath the graffiti. From the stone parapets on the fortress walls, you can imagine what it was like to defend the town against invaders.

Across from the fort entrance is the town's **Archaeological Museum.** Its worthy collection of local artefacts gives a good overview of Minoan pottery, figurines, seal stones, jewellery, and bronzework for those who haven't the time to visit larger museums. There are wonderful clay sarcophagi with animal and geometric motifs from Minoan cemeteries found in the area.

Below the fortress is the attractive **inner harbour,** lined with seafood tavernas and an old lighthouse on the jetty. Beyond it, the palm-lined waterfront **promenade** runs east along the shore; the tourist office shares a small building with the tourist police halfway along to the breakwater.

Plunge into the **old town** along Odós Paleológou. Just past the Venetian loggia on bustling Platía Petiháki is the **Rimondi Fountain** (1629), with lion's-head waterspouts crowning Corinthian columns. Nearby on Vernardou is the **Djamí ton Neranzión** (Nerantzes Mosque), now a concert hall; there are great views from its minaret. Farther along is the **Historical and Folk Art Museum.**

Head up Ethníkis Antistáseos, the market street, to **Porta Guora,** the Venetian gateway. Beyond are the **municipal gardens,** where the wine festival is held each July. Wander back through the old town and lose yourself in the narrow alleyways, admiring the Venetian stone façades with their barred windows and arched doorways; the overhanging, closed wooden balconies were added by the Turks.

Odós Arkadíou is the main shopping street, though tiny Souliou, behind the loggia, is much more interesting. The **Kanakakis Gallery,** a centre for contemporary art, is situated below the fortress on Mesologgiou near the Catholic Church. Beyond the old town are two more mosques (both closed). Little **Kara Pasha**, near Platía Iróon, has a pretty garden, while the larger **Veli Pasha** and its minaret stand abandoned in a field, to the south of the town hall along Odós Zimvrakaki.

The North Coast Beaches

East of Réthimnon, the wide, sandy beach extends for some 25 km (16 miles). The coast road runs through a ribbon of well-developed resort towns to Stavromenos, where the road joins the National Highway. Facilities range from simple rooms and studios to luxury hotels offering every amenity. The next major resort is **Bali,** with a pretty location but too many buildings clustered in the hills around small coves. Although ambitiously developed, **Agía Pelagía,** spread out along the inlets of a deep-blue headland bay off the Gulf of Iráklion, is very attractive and offers excellent swimming.

There are several inviting, undeveloped stretches of sand to the west of Réthimnon along Almirós Bay, but note that there are also dangerous currents here, and swimmers should avoid venturing far offshore. The pretty village of **Georgióupolis** has become a small resort and offers a rather safer area for swimming near the breakwater close to town. Across the headland towards Soúda Bay, **Almirída** and the larger market town of **Kalíves** are both attractive spots with some good beaches, tavernas, and low-key tourism. They are especially popular with local families.

Arkádi Monastery and Beyond

Perched on a rugged mountainside southeast of Réthimnon, the 16th-century **Moní Arkadíou** (Arkádi Monastery) is one of the most revered sites of the Cretan struggle for independence. In 1866 it became an armed bastion of revolt, with hundreds of villagers taking refuge within its walls. Rather than surrender to besieging Turkish troops, Abbot Gabriel waited for them to storm the monastery and then blew up the gunpowder magazine, killing hundreds of soldiers and nearly 1,000 villagers. His action forever symbolized the Cretan motto—"Freedom or death."

The monastery has since been restored, though the refectory is still pockmarked with bullet holes. The handsome church here is among the finest surviving Venetian structures on the island. You may recognize its decorative façade—it's printed on the 100-drachma note. A **museum** preserves relics of the suicidal massacre, while a mausoleum displays the victims' bones.

A new paved road from Arkádi leads to the ancient site of **Eleftherná.** Apart from a tower there are few significant remains of the Doric city-state (seventh-eighth centuries B.C.), but the stunning setting atop a ridge is worth seeing. The quaint village of **Margarítes,** farther along the road, is a popular stop for its pottery workshops.

Northeast of Pérama, the **Melidóni Cave** is another important shrine to Cretan independence. In 1824, some 300 villagers took refuge here. When they refused to surrender, the Turkish troops blocked the air passages and set fires at

The handsome church of the Arkádi Monastery is among one of the finest buildings in Crete.

the mouth of the cave, asphyxiating everyone inside. The vast domed cavern with incredible stalactites and stalagmites is a moving memorial.

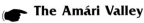

The Amári Valley

The drive along the western slopes of Mount Ida takes you through bewitching countryside. The sharp curves can surprise you, however, so take it at a slow pace. Starting east of Réthimnon, the Amári road winds up through ancient olive groves and meadows filled with wild flowers in springtime, with awesome views of Psilorítis (see page 49) popping into view.

After Apostoli, take the valley's left fork up the hill to **Thrónos.** The 14th-century **Panagía chapel,** with lovely frescoes, stands on a terrace that still bears traces of mosaics from an Early Christian basilica. From the south side of town an easy climb takes you to the acropolis of the ancient Greek town of **Sybrita.**

At the Venetian Asomáton Monastery, now an agricultural college, the Amári road turns right to **Monastiráki;** its church, like that of **Opsigiás,** has some noteworthy frescoes. **Amári,** the valley's main village, boasts the island's oldest frescoes (1225) in the chapel of St. Anna, which stands in a meadow on the outskirts of town. The town's steep lanes, with their red-tiled roofs and a Venetian clock tower, are delightful to explore.

At **Vizari,** there are remains of an Early Christian basilica outside of town. The Panagía church at **Platanía** has more 15th-century frescoes. Continue down just past **Fourfourás** for a view across the Messará Plain. Shortly beyond, you can turn right and head back up the western flank of the valley, also very scenic. The villages around here were burned by German troops during World War II, but several frescoed churches have survived.

The South Coast

The quickest way to the south coast is on the good road from Réthimnon to Agía Galíni. Along the way, stop off at the small mountain town of **Spíli** to see the Venetian fountain, with water pouring out of a long row of lion heads. The steep cobbled streets above the square are perfect for wandering as they meander past white-washed old houses bedecked with lush foliage.

The next up-and-coming resort is **Plakiás,** to the west of Spíli, still fairly small and strung along a windy beach of coarse sand. To get here you go through the **Kourtaliótiko Gorge,** home to Lammergeier vultures and other birds of prey soaring high above the towering cliffs.

Just east of Plakiás, the **Moní Préveli** (Préveli Monastery) sits atop a barren mountain plateau. In World War II, the monks helped evacuate Allied troops after the Battle of Crete (see page 25). The church and grounds contain memorials to this event, as well as a museum of relics and icons. On the way up, you pass the evocative ruins of the earlier **St. John's monastery** (16th century). A rough track leads down to Préveli's much-touted **Palm Beach,** though it is more easily reached by boat.

From Plakiás, a rough but scenic mountain road provides a tortuous westward route, with vistas over the coastline. It passes through isolated villages and emerges onto a flat coastal plain. From here, the dark gorges slicing the stark granite walls of the coastal range are easily visible.

Only the huge shell remains of the 14th-century fortress of **Frangokástello,** which guards a quiet, shallow beach of hard-packed sand. Around 17 May, when eerie dawn mists surround the castle, Cretans claim to see the ghosts of a band of freedom fighters who died here when they took a stand against the Turks in 1828.

About 12 km (7 miles) west is the port of **Chóra Sfakíon,** hemmed in between the mountains and the sea. Further coastal travel is only possible by boat. Harbour restaurants cater to the boatloads of day-trippers visiting the Samariá Gorge (see page 70). Other trips go to Gávdos, Crete's largest offshore island, and west to **Paleochóra** (see p.75). If you get a chance, visit the picture-perfect village of **Loutro.**

The hair-raising road north from Chóra Sfakíon leads to the village of **Imbros.** An 11-km (7-mile) trek through the gorge to Kommitades offers the same fine scenery as the Samariá Gorge, but with a gentler descent. Before you rejoin the National Highway, stop at **Vrísses** to try what is said to be Crete's best yoghurt.

The Samariá Gorge

Crete's most famous natural wonder is the **Samariá Gorge,** which begins on the Omalós Plateau, 11,000 metres (3,609 feet) up in the White Mountains. Its awesome beauty shelters ancient cypresses, rare orchids and plants, and the Cretan wild goat, or *kri-kri.* Formed by a river that rushes some 18 km (11 miles) to the sea, it is the longest gorge in Europe. You can hike it from May to October, weather permitting, when the torrent dries up to a trickling stream. Note that "weather" often refers to high winds, which close the gorge because of the danger of falling rocks.

Perhaps the most amazing thing about the gorge is the number of visitors determined to make the strenuous 16-km (10-mile) trek. On no account underestimate the stamina required, especially in the summer. It's straight down all the way, over a rocky path that becomes an exhausting slog after the first few exhilarating miles. The sun beats down relentlessly, and there are long stretches with little shade. Solid footwear that can withstand sharp rocks is essential, as are a

The breathtaking view of nature's Samariá Gorge.

hat, sunglasses, and sun screen. Spring water is available at six rest-points along the trail, but take a bottle you can refill.

The easy way to see the gorge is to journey by boat from Chóra Sfakíon to **Agía Rouméli** and then explore the lower half in the early morning. If you're up for a serious hike, you can drive or take the bus from Chaniá to **Omalós,** 42 km (26 miles), or join the multitude of guided tours. The hike down to Agía Rouméli takes between five and seven hours; there, you catch a boat to Chóra Sfakíon to meet the bus (or pre-arranged taxi) for the return.

Park wardens give you a ticket (1,500drs), to be surrendered at the other end to ensure that no one is left stranded in the gorge at the end of the day. The descent begins with a **xilóskalon** (wooden staircase). With the wall of Mount Gíngilos towering above, the stone path drops sharply away in a series of switchbacks, falling 1,000 metres (3,280 feet) in the first couple of kilometres. Take it easy and keep to the path.

The route becomes less steep once you reach the rest point at the **chapel of Ágios Nikólaos,** 4 km (2½ miles) on. Baby *kri-kri*, less timid than their parents, sometimes venture down to this shady spot. The cool, clear pools are inviting, but swimming is strictly forbidden. The abandoned village of **Samariá,** with its 14th-century church of Ossia Maria (Mary's Bones), marks the halfway point. There's a warden's post and first-aid station here; if you're truly in distress you can be taken out by mule.

Beyond is the gorge's narrowest point, the **Sideróportes** (Iron Gates), only 3.5 metres (11 feet) wide but 300 metres (1,000 feet) high. From here the gorge opens up in its approach to the sea. The final stretch through the shadeless riverbed is perhaps the most gruelling in very hot weather..

☛ Chaniá

Crete's second largest city and former capital, **Chaniá,** can lay claim to the loveliest urban waterfront on the island. In fact, many Greeks and non-Greeks alike consider Chaniá to be the most beautiful city in all of Greece. Like Réthimnon, its old quarter presents an evocative legacy of Venetian and Turkish influences. Driving—and parking—in the narrow lanes can be a nightmare, however, and it's less stressful to arrive by bus. Chaniá's sand beaches lie to the west of town, with the best ones at Golden Beach and farther on at Kalamáki.

The covered **market hall** on Platía S. Venizélou marks the separation of the old and new parts of town. Shaped liked a cross, its four "arms" display a wealth of Cretan produce. This is a good place to find Cretan dittany (*díktamus*), which is used for a medicinal herb tea. You can also have lunch with the traders in the small food stalls serving Cretan dishes.

Nearby is Odós Skridlóf, or Leather Street, with some of the best leather goods in Crete. This part of town, down to the waterfront, is the old Jewish **Evréïka quarter.**

A vaulted Venetian church on Odós Hálidon provides the impressive setting for the **Archaeological Museum.** Its highlights include marvellous third-century Roman mosaics, Linear A and B tablets from Kastélli, and an intricate scene of an ancient Minoan town inscribed on a seal stone called the *Master Impression*. Inside the courtyard of the Catholic church next door is the entrance to the small **Cretan Folklore Museum.**

The grand loop of the Venetian harbour is ringed with medieval buildings. Viewed at sunset from the lighthouse, at the end of the long breakwater of golden stone, the lights of the shops, cafés, and tavernas make up one of the most enchanting images on the whole island.

At the western tip is the **Firkás,** a restored section of the Venetian ramparts, housing the **Naftikó Mousío** (Naval Museum), with displays including ancient Greek ship models. Facing it across the harbour is Chaniá's oldest Turkish building, the **Djamí ton Genissarión** (Mosque of the Janissaries) (1645), now a tourist information centre.

Few would guess at Chaniá's violent past from its beautiful, serene harbourfront today.

The ancient Minoan city of Kydonía is buried beneath the **Kastélli quarter** behind the mosque. Scant remains have been found to date, suggesting it was not a city of high status, but many believe there's a Minoan palace still to be discovered. Kydonía later came into its own and flourished in the classical Greek, Roman and Byzantine years. The Venetians centred their city of La Canea here, but its remains were largely destroyed during World War II bombardment.

Farther along the waterfront are seven of the original 17 **arsenali**, where the Venetians built and repaired their ships. Behind them the cobbled lanes of the atmospheric **Splánzia quarter** lead to the **church of Ágios Nikólaos**, ecumenically sporting a Venetian Catholic bell-tower and Turkish Moslem minaret. Or continue on around the inner harbour and along the sea wall to the lighthouse—a hefty walk.

Head up Zambelíou to explore the narrow streets of the Turkish **Topanás quarter** behind the Firkás. The houses have old Venetian stone facades with wooden upper storeys added on by the Turks. Crumbling houses and chapels lurk behind weatherbeaten gates. Odós Theotokopoúlou, through the Renieri Gate on Moshon, has local craftware.

☞ Soúda and Akrotíri

The strategic harbour of Soúda Bay serves Chaniá-bound passengers on the overnight ferry from Piraeus (Athens' port). Measuring 15 km (9 miles) in length and 16 km (10 miles) across in parts, this is one of the best deep-water ports in the Mediterranean Sea. Much of the harbour serves as a naval base for the Greek navy and its NATO allies. The long green slope at the head of the bay is the British War Cemetery for soldiers killed in Crete during World War II.

On **Akrotíri**, the peninsula to the east of Chaniá, the tomb of Greek Prime Minister Elefthérios Venizélos (see page 25) lies on the hill of Profítis Ilías, where Cretan insurgents demanding *énosis* (union) first raised the flag of Greece in 1897 in defiance of the European powers. There is a panoramic view over the gulf.

Drive through the cheerful countryside to see three monasteries. The 17th-century **Agía Triáda** is a major pilgrimage centre. From the older **Moní Gouvernétou** further on, you can hike down to the derelict monastery of **Katholikó**; the caves here were inhabited by pagan and Christian hermits.

The Far West

The Gulf of Chaniá west of town is the most developed part of western Crete. A continuous ribbon of hotels runs along the coast to Kolimbári. Some of the best beaches and watersports are at **Agía Marína** and **Plataniás**, which also has an attractive old quarter. **Máleme** is where the German invasion of Crete began in 1941, and there is a well-tended German war cemetery here.

Beyond **Kastélli Kissámou**, Crete's western coast is still very remote. The wonderful beach on the long curving bay of **Falásarna**, however, is one of the best on the island, reached via a good road from Plátanos. Remains of the ancient port city are scattered over the cliffs.

On the south coast, the busy little port town of **Paleochóra** has a broad sandy beach, plenty of accommodation and lively tavernas. It is a good base for excursions to the coral pink beaches of Elafoníssi island, or Gávdos.

The main road south to Paleochóra lies west of Máleme, but a more scenic route begins on the outskirts of Chaniá, by way of **Perivolia**. You'll notice immediately the lush vegetation of western Crete. Extensive orange groves line the roadside around **Skinés**, bearing fruit well into the winter. As you climb into mountains there are great clumps of wild basil, oregano and thyme sprouting from the rocky soil. The steady ascent culminates in a dramatic mountain pass before winding down towards the coast, turning left for the pebbly beach at **Soúgia** and right towards Paleochóra.

EXCURSION TO SANTORINI

The Cycladic island of Santorini, also known as Thíra, is dramatically linked to Crete. The volcanic explosion here around 1450 B.C.—five times greater than that of Krakatoa —rocked the ancient world, and is believed to have brought about the catastrophic destruction of the Minoan civilization on Crete, 44 km (70 miles) due south. Some scholars believe that the island is part of the legendary lost continent of Atlantis. Indeed, the whole centre of Thíra sank under the sea in that prehistoric eruption. Greece's last active volcano still smoulders today, and the caldera is ringed with the small Burnt Isles that rose again in more recent eruptions.

Cruise ships sail to Santorini from the major resorts and make for a popular day trip. In summer there are several ferries each week from Iráklion. But you'll find there's much to explore, and this small island repays a longer stay.

The magic of Santorini begins as soon as you sail into the caldera. Sheer cliffs rise over 300 metres (1,000 feet) above the sea, exposing stark volcanic layers of red and brown. What looks from afar like snowcapped mountains turns out to be a chain of whitewashed buildings clinging to the ridgetops. Most cruise ships dock at the port of **Skala**, below the capital, Thíra. Inter-island ferries land at the newer port of Athinios, a short bus or taxi ride away.

A steep flight of 588 broad stone steps zig-zags up to the town. Mule teams are standing by to take you to the top in the traditional way. A funicular lift provides a smoother, faster ride. **Thíra** is far more appealing from a distance. It's a touristy place, jammed with jewellery shops, travel agents and pricy café-bars, and it gets very crowded in high season. But make your way to the path along the cliff for stunning views back across the town and you'll fall under Santorini's spell once more. There's a small archaeological museum, and boat trips out to the volcano, where you can scramble around the desolate hills of lava rocks with their sulphurous fumes.

Picturesque **Oía** (Ia) to the north is more rewarding than Thíra. The town is a showpiece for Santorini's splendid barrel-vault architecture. The island's famous sunsets are unforgettable here, looking out over the blue-domed churches to the fiery red ball sinking behind the caldera.

In 1967 excavations began at **Akrotíri**, revealing a rich Minoan town on the southwest finger of the island. A sense of discovery prevails at this dig-in-progress under a vast iron roof. The houses are remarkably intact, with walls up to three storeys high, fireplaces, and handsome door and window frames. Exquisite frescoes were found here, though they are now in Athens' National Archaeological Museum until a new museum can be built for them on site. No lava mummies were found in this Minoan Pompeii, suggesting that the ancient islanders may have had enough warning to evacuate before the explosion.

Inland, Santorini's other 12 villages are surrounded by fields of rich volcanic soil that produce tomatoes and grapes for the island's good wines. Note how the vines are curled into baskets so that the grapes fall into the centre. **Pirgos** is a lovely village on the way to the monastery atop the summit of **Profítis Ilías**. On the promontory dividing the beach resorts of Kamári and Períssa lie the ruins of **Ancient Thíra**, a third-century garrison town for the Ptolemies. Below are the fine black sand beaches that make Santorini the "black pearl of the Aegean."

Museum Highlights

Hours are correct at the time of printing, but should be checked with the tourist office. All museums have reduced admission for students.

Palace of Knossós

The Palace of Knossós is near Iráklion. 5 km (3 miles) south on marked road. The largest of the Miman palaces (and most famous of all Minoan sites), built around 1700 B.C. Open Tues-Fri 8am-5pm, Sat-Sun 8:30am-3pm. Admission fee. (see page 39)

Archaeological Museum, Iráklion.

Platía Eleftherías; tel. (081) 226092. One of the most important museums in Greece, which housing the finest collection of Minoan artefacts. Open Tues-Fri 8am-7pm, Mon 12:30pm– 5pm; weekends 8:30am–3:30pm. Admission fee. (See page 34)

Museum of Religious Art, Iráklion.

Platía Agías Ekaterínis. Six master paintings by Damaskinós, icons, frescoes and other works of medieval religious art. Open Mon-Sat 9am-1:30pm and Tues, Thurs, Fri 5-8pm. Admission fee. (See page 32)

Historical and Ethnological Museum, Iráklion.

Odós S. Venizélou; tel. (081) 283219. Exhibits from the Byzantine, Venetian and Turkish periods and recent history. Folk art, costumes, textiles. Open Tues-Sun 8am-3pm. Admission fee. (See page 34

Archaeological Museum, Ágios Nikólaos.

The Archaeological Museum is in Odós Paleologou; tel. (0841) 24943. Minoan and other artefacts from regional sites in eastern Crete. Open Tues-Sun 8:30am-3pm. Admission fee. (See page 54)

Archaeological Museum, Sitía.
On the lerápetra road. Regional artefacts and finds from the Minoan palace at Káto Zákros. Open Tues-Sat 8:30am-3pm, Sun 9:30am-2pm. Admission fee. (See page 60)

Phaistós
Phaistós is near Gortyna; tel. (0892) 22615. Another beautiful Minoan palace, built around 1650 B.C. Open daily 8am-7pm. Admission fee. (see page 46)

Archaeological Museum, Réthimnon.
The Archaeological Museum is opposite the entrance to the Venetian fortress; tel. (0831) 29975. Good collection of Minoan finds from the region. Open Tues-Sun 8:30am-3pm. Admission fee. (See page 65)

Archaeological Museum, Chaniá.
The Archaelogical Museum is in Odós Hálidon; tel. (0821) 20334. Housed in the Venetian church of San Francesco. Exhibits from western Crete, from the Neolithic to Roman era. Open Mon-Fri 8am-5pm, Sat-Sun 8:30am-3pm. Admission fee. (See page 73)

Naval Museum of Crete, Chaniá.
The Naval Museum is in the Firkás; tel. (0821) 26437. Ship models and naval memorabilia from Classical times to the present; seashell collection. Open daily 10am-4pm. Admission fee. (See page 73)

CRETE

SEA OF CRETE

LIBYAN SEA

To Rhodes
To Santorini (Thira)
To Piraeus
To Antikíthira-Kíthira

Legend:
- Regional border
- Main road
- Motorway
- Ferry route
- Place of interest

Falásarna
Kastélli
Kissámou
Kolimbári
Maleme Plátanas
Marina
Agia
Moni Gonía
Perivólia
Chaniá
Kalíves
M
Almirída
Georgioúpolis
Plaka
Almiros Bay
Gulf of Chaniá
AKROTÍRI
Moni Katholikó
Moni Gouvernétou
Omalós
Lefká Óri (White Mountains)
Samariá
Órmos Páralia Samariá
Agia Roumeli
Loutró
Chóra Sfakíon
Frangokástello
Sougiá
Palaeochóra
Elafonísi Island
Gávdos
Imbros
Spíli
Moni Préveli
Plakiás
Rethímnon
Stavromenos
Bali
Melidóni Cave
Garázo
Margarítes
Moni Arkadíou
Amári
Anógia
Amári Valley
Agía Galíni
Timbáki
Festós
Matála
Messará Bay
Agía Triáda
Fourfourás
Psilorítis
Zarós
Kamáres
Kamáres Cave
Nída Plateau
Mt Psilorítis
Goris
Vóri
Mires
Agii Déka
Górtys
Asteroússia Mountains
Agia Pelagia
Fódele
Amoudára
Iráklion
Gázi
Knossós
Tílissos
Anópoli
Profítis Ilías
Ag. Varvára
Kastélli
Hersónissos (Liménes Hersonissou)
Mália
Limin
Amnísos
Skotinó Cave
Tzermiádo
Psychró
Diktéan Ántron (Diktean Cave)
Lasíthi (Dikti) Mountains
Myrtos
Elóunda
Oloús
Spinalónga
Mirabéllo Bay
Agios Nikólaos
Néapoli
Kritsá
Kalamáfka
Gourniá
Istro
Pahiá Ámmos
Ierápetra
Mochlós
Agia Fotiá
Makrigialós
Análipsi
Siteía
Vái
Móni Toploú
Zákros
Palékastro
Káto Zákros
Dia
Chrissi Island

0   40 km
0   20 miles

N

WHAT TO DO

SHOPPING

The large towns and resorts around the island have a multitude of shops where you'll find a range of Cretan crafts and souvenirs. Best buys to look for include weaving and embroidery, leather goods, pottery, jewellery, and knitwear. It's worth shopping around to get a good idea of prices and quality. In the villages and some town shops you can try bargaining, especially if you buy more than one item, but keep in mind the skill and materials involved, and the fact that the local profit margins have to cover the off season when the shop is closed.

Souvenirs

There's plenty of kitsch about, although you can occasionally find good museum copies of classical Greek statues and fine handmade dolls in traditional costume. Greek worry beads (*kombolóïa*) make interesting souvenirs—look for those made from olive-wood with bright tassels. Carefully hand-carved wooden spoons, bowls, and statues are popular

> **Items marked EKPTWSEIS are on sale.**

gifts, as are *bríkia*, the long-stemmed copper coffee pots used to make Greek coffee. The fringed, crocheted headscarves worn by men in traditional costume, and curved Cretan knives with decorative silver scabbards, make excellent mementoes.

Antiques and Icons

Antiques that predate Greek independence in 1821 require an export permit, which is practically impossible to acquire for anything truly ancient. Small items such as coins, terracotta, or bronze figurines, and supposedly genuine Byzantine icons, are likely to be fake anyway. The best place to find good replicas or modern icons in a traditional style is in the museum shops and monasteries, though they are expensive. For further information on exporting antiques, see Customs and Entry Formalities on page 108.

Textiles and Leather

Crete is well known for its beautiful fabrics. Many villages still have working looms that produce attractive rugs, blankets, wall-hangings, and shoulder bags; materials range from fine grades to coarse goat hair. You can also buy the material by the roll and have it shipped home.

Cretan weaving, known as *hyfanda*, is based on traditional designs handed down from mother to daughter. Embroidery and lacework is also outstanding. Some of the finest work (and best prices) can be found in the villages of Kritsá and Anógia.

Leather boots, shoes, and sandals are still handmade in the villages of western Crete. Many of the shops in Réthimnon and

Chaniá's "Leather Street" abound with fine belts, handbags and rucksacks, and you'll almost always be offered a better price than the one marked.

Jewellery and Ceramics

Jewellery styles are often dictated by ancient designs; you will see delicate Minoan

Sparkling jewellery in a Chaniá storefront window.

spirals and replicas of the famous honeybee pendant on display in Iráklion's Archaeological Museum. Gold and silver are generally cheaper in Greece. They are sold by weight (each item should be weighed in front of you), while any workmanship and creativity involves additional cost. Some gold rings are made from two different purities—before you buy, check for hollowness and make sure that the correct weight–price equivalents are being used. There is an abundance of jewellery shops on the island, with the best selection possibly to be found in Iráklion near the Archaeological Museum.

Like their ancient ancestors, Cretans are excellent potters. Ceramic vases and pots often replicate ancient patterns and styles. In Iráklion you can purchase direct from the workshops. Chaniá is known for its blue clay pottery. In the village of Margarítes you can watch the craftsmen at work.

Edible Gifts

Browse in the markets for wild herbs picked in the mountains: basil, thyme, oregano, and saffron. You can make herbal tea from Cretan dittany (*díktamus*), a medicinal plant used since ancient times to heal arrow wounds and cure a variety of ills; it's also reputed to be an aphrodisiac. Delicious Cretan thyme honey is sold in small jars or by the kilo; the darker, cold-pressed variety is

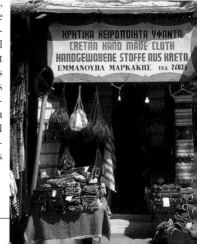

There's always a find in one of the many souvenir shops.

best, made in the traditional manner. The island's olive oil is also considered to be one of the finest in Greece.

SPORTS

Crete's coastal resorts and mountainous interior provide arenas for all kinds of activities besides swimming. Perhaps the best way to enjoy the island is simply to walk in the countryside and admire the views, particularly in springtime, when flowers abound.

Swimming

The seas are warm enough for swimming from May to mid-October. With approximately 24,000 km (15,000 miles) of coastline, the island has scores of beaches to choose from. Note that the ideal beach is not always the one with the finest sand—pebble beaches are preferable for days when the strong *méltemi* wind is blowing. Rock-ledge beaches are generally uncrowded, but you should wear plastic sandals to paddle around on the rocks.

For children, make sure you have some really safe, shallow bathing available, as lifeguards are very rare. Everyone should obey the safety warning flags posted on the beach. Just remember the traffic lights: red means dangerous conditions, orange or yellow mean "swim with caution," green or white mean "go on in, the water's fine." There are dangerous offshore currents in many places on the north coast, such as at Georgióupolis, Amoudára, and Mália. Listen to local advice and don't swim out too far.

Nudist bathing is officially forbidden, but in practice you will find a number of beaches where people take it all off. The criterion seems to be the more secluded places not frequented by families or by the Greeks themselves—take care not to offend.

Boating and Fishing

The major resorts all rent out boats and other equipment, and even in the tiniest fishing harbour you should find a caïque to hire, though the island's unpredictable winds can make sailing somewhat hazardous and frustrating. Boat trips along the coast and to offshore islands are offered at most resorts.

Shore fishing or from a boat you can catch seabass, swordfish, dentex, and a host of other fish. No special licence is needed, but underwater spear fishing is restricted.

Curious "locals" are eager to join in the fun at Vai beach in eastern Crete.

Watersports

All of the main resort beaches provide equipment for waterskiing, jet-skiing, windsurfing, and often paragliding. The beaches at Almirída and Paleochóra are popular with windsurfers, and there is a good windsurfing centre in Plaka, near Eloúnda.

Scuba diving is restricted to designated areas where you cannot disturb underwater archaeological sites. Diving centres include the Barracuda Club and the Crete Watersports Centre in Agía Pelagía, and The Divers in Plakiás. Snorkelling is allowed everywhere, and the submerged ruins of Oloús at Eloúnda and Móchlos on Mirabéllo Bay are fun to explore.

Biking

Mountain biking is an exciting way to see the island. Bike touring centres at Amoudára, Réthimnon, and other resorts rent equipment and offer bike treks for all ability levels.

Hiking and Climbing

The old bridlepaths across the island make marvellous walking routes. There are challenging gorge walks through the Samariá, Imbros, and Rouvas gorges. Hikers must take care when venturing into the high mountains, as it is easy to get lost and water can be scarce.

The Hellenic Alpine Club (EOS), with branches in Iráklion, Réthimnon, and Chaniá, organizes hiking outings into the mountains. Foreigners are welcome to join and the local tourist office will give you details. The club is also a good source for mountain guides. More ambitious climbers aiming at Mount Ida or peaks in the White Mountains can ask about guides and equipment at the Greek Federation of Mountaineering Associations in Chaniá. It operates mountain refuges and has produced a leaflet on a new hiking route across the island.

Tennis

Most big resort hotels have hard courts. Chaniá and Iráklion both have tennis clubs, and there are public courts in Iráklion behind the Archaeological Museum.

ENTERTAINMENT

Hotels and restaurants in the resort areas regularly put on Cretan evenings of traditional-style entertainment to give their guests a taste of the island's music, dancing, and costumes. To find the real thing, however, you must explore the mountain villages. A saint's feast day or a wedding is always cause for festivities, and such occasions are celebrated with throbbing rhythms and forceful melodies. Throughout the summer, almost each village hosts a *panayiraie* (celebration) to hear its patron saint; this an excellent way to experience Cretan Song and dance, as well as the warmth of village life (local tourist boards can provide a schedule of these celebrations).

Symphonic and choral performances are held at Réthimnon's summer arts festivals. In the summer, films are shown in open-air cinemas, presented in their original version and subtitled in Greek.

Cretan Music

Crete's main musical instrument is the *lyra*, a U-shaped stringed instrument. Others include the *laouto*, a kind of mandolin; the *askomantoura*, Cretan bagpipes; and the *habioli*, or shepherd's flute. You'll also hear the *bouzoúki*, a long-necked Turkish import that is now popular all over Greece.

Cretan folk songs tend towards the lyrical, sentimental, and expressive—with forceful melodies. The *mantinada* consists of rhyming couplets that are passed down through the generations or sometimes improvised; they have dramatic themes of love, death, and human emotions. *Rizítika* are patriotic or heroic songs of the western mountains.

The *syrtáki* dance popularized in the film *Zorba the Greek* is actually a hybrid of several distinct dances, but it's the one you'll most often see at the resort Greek nights. It begins with the man swaying slowly, arms outstretched, taking long steps sideways or forwards, and making a twisting leap before retrieving his more deliberate rhythm. This blossoms into the *khassápikos*, or butcher's dance, with two or three men joining arms.

In characteristic Cretan folk dances, the dancers form a chain and all join in. Some of the most common are the slow, majestic *tsamíko* dance of the mountain rebels; the *syrtós* circle dance; the *soústa* hop-dance from Réthimnon; and the high-spirited *pendozalis*.

CRETE FOR CHILDREN

Crete is a popular holiday spot for families, and most resorts are happy to cater for children. Many larger hotels have separate, shallow children's swimming pools and play areas, and some of the large ones offer special games and activity programmes. Greeks love children, and yours will be welcome at restaurants and tavernas.

In the hills above Hersónissos, **Aqua Splash** is a water park with slides and a hydrotube. In Chaniá, young ones

will enjoy a horse-and-buggy ride around the harbour; while in Réthimnon they can tour the old town on a tram train.

Area children dress in traditional costume for a parade.

Calendar of Events

1 January: St. Basil's Day (*Protochroniá*)—a sprig of basil offered is a symbol of hospitality.

6 January: Epiphany (*ton Theofaníon*)—young men dive to retrieve a cross thrown into the harbour in coastal towns.

February: The two weeks before Lent (*Apókries*) are celebrated with carnivals in Iráklion and Réthimnon.

Clean Monday (*Katharí Deftéra*): The first day of Lent—picnics and kite-flying before the abstinence begins.

25 March: Independence Day—Parades and dancing commemorate the revolt against the Turks in 1821.

Orthodox Easter: Candlelit processions follow a flower-bedecked bier on Good Friday (*Megáli Paraskeví*). On Holy Saturday, Judas is burned in effigy, fireworks are let off, and at midnight the priest passes the sacred flame from candle to candle for each household to light an oil lamp. On Sunday (*Páscha*), lambs are sacrificed for roasting, as in ancient Greece at the beginning of spring.

20-27 May: Chaniá commemorates the Battle of Crete with music and dancing.

24 June: Feast of St. John the Baptist and Summer Solstice—bonfires are lit across the island and young boys jump over the embers.

July/August: Iráklion Festival of cultural events; wine festival and Renaissance Festival in Réthimnon; wine festival in Sitía; *lyra* music festival in Anógia.

15 August: Assumption Day (*tis Panangías*)—Dancing, fireworks and craft fairs at Móchlos (near Mália) and Neápolis.

28 October: *Óchi* ('No') Day—Parade in Réthimnon celebrates Greek defiance of surrender ultimatum in 1940.

7-9 November: Anniversary of 1866 explosion at Arkádi; festivities at the monastery and in Réthimnon.

11 November: Feast of St. Mínas, Iráklion's patron saint.

EATING OUT

One of the most pleasant experiences on Crete is the evening meal, perhaps eaten *al fresco* by the waterfront or in a leafy courtyard garden. The excellent natural ingredients at the heart of Greek cuisine have hardly changed since ancient times: fresh grilled fish, charcoal-grilled meats, delicious olives, oil and lemon, flavoured with garlic, wild thyme, basil, and oregano.

The best Cretan cooking is wholesome, hearty, and unpretentious, served with small touches that reveal the Greek appreciation for the simple joys of life. When choosing a restaurant, don't judge on appearance. Often the most basic places offer the best quality, and good food is better value than a stylish table setting. Try, whenever possible, to go where the Cretans go. In the coastal resorts, for instance, the islanders often keep away from the crowded harbourside establishments. In the backstreet tavernas, you can enjoy the real zing of a full garlicky *dzadzíki*, not watered down for tourist palates.

Most restaurants in resort areas have made some concessions to the tourist trade, and the less adventurous diner can generally order an omelette, pizza, spaghetti, or chips. At tourist restaurants menus are usually printed in English, German, and French as well as Greek. But only a fraction of the tantalizing Greek specialities listed may be available at any one time—only those items with a price beside them are being served that day.

There's no need to puzzle over what an entrée entails: most restaurants in the tourist areas have photos of their various dishes displayed on the back of the menu, if not on a board alongside the pavement. Or do as the locals do: In most Greek restaurants it's common practice to enter the kitchen, inspect the dishes of the day, and point out those you'd like to try. A half-portion is *olígo* (a little).

Portions are generally substantial. An appetizer such as a plate of calamari and a Greek salad will make a satisfactory meal if you're eating light.

To attract the waiter's attention, call *parakaló* (please). The service charge is included in the bill, but diners normally leave between 5 and 10 per cent extra as a tip. Before starting their meal, Greeks will wish each other *kalí órexi* (bon appetit).

Appetizers (Mezédes)

It is the Greek custom to eat appetizers (*mezédes*), accompanied by an aperitif of *oúzo* and water, separately from the main meal. For convenience's sake, *mezédes* are usually served at resort tavernas as part of the dinner. But the essence of the *meze* is really its leisurely enjoyment, something to savour for itself. It is possible to make a whole meal just from the *mezédes*, but go easy on the quantities — some of the dishes are particularly rich for the unaccustomed stomach.

Be sure to try some of these Cretan favourites: *dzadzíki* (a yoghurt dip with crushed garlic and grated or

An outdoor cafe in the village of Kritsá is a great place to take a break.

finely sliced cucumber, served chilled and with bread); *taramosaláta* (a creamy pink paste of cod's roe mixed with mashed potatoes or breadcrumbs, egg yolk, lemon juice, and olive oil); *dolmádes* (vine leaves filled with rice and pine kernels, or minced meat, and served cold—make sure they're fresh and not from a tin!); *kalamarákia* (small squid, fried in batter and served with a slice of lemon); *tirópitakia* (pastries of goat and ewe cheese); *salingária* (Cretan snails); and, of course, dishes of olives.

Soups

Cretan soups of *fakés* (lentil), *revíthia* (chickpea), or *fasólia* (bean) are excellent. Seafood restaurants may keep going a cauldron of *psarósoupa* (fish soup) or *kalamariáki* (spicy squid and tomato). Don't miss the chance to try the famous Greek soup *avgolémono* (egg and lemon with chicken broth, thickened with rice), if it's on the menu.

Greek Specialities

Saláta choriátiki (a "village salad" of tomatoes, cucumbers, onions, and green peppers topped with *féta* cheese and black olives) is standard throughout Greece and simply called "Greek salad." *Moussaká* (layers of sliced aubergine and minced lamb baked with a white sauce and grated cheese) is one of the most popular of Greek dishes. *Pastítsio* (minced meat and macaroni with white sauce and cheese) can be eaten as either a first or main course.

Fish and Seafood

Fresh fish, though expensive, is one of the finest pleasures of the Greek table. Go down to the harbour to see what has been caught that day. At the restaurant, you will often be invited into the kitchen to select your own. Remember that fish

is priced by weight, so the size you choose becomes your re-
sponsibility when the bill arrives.

Xifías (swordfish), generally frozen and often served on the
skewer, is very good value. *Barboúnia* (red mullet), *glóssa*
(sole), and *lithríni* (bream) are
among the most popular. *Sardéles*
(sardines) are excellent baked,
while *marídes* (whitebait) are
served fried. And you'll come

> Before ordering,
> stroll into the kitchen
> and have a look at
> what's cooking.

across a host of other Greek fish that have no simple English
translations.

The "lobster" proposed on some menus is almost invariably
a clawless crustacean properly known as crayfish or rock lobster. If you like your seafood stewed, try octopus with white
wine, tomatoes, and potatoes, or *garídes* (prawns) in white
wine and *féta* cheese.

Meat Dishes

You'll find *souvlákia* (marinated lamb or veal kebabs) everywhere around the island. It is served in tavernas, often with a
combination plate, and in *psistariás* (snack bars), which also
offer *gyros* (slices of meat from spitroasted cones of pork,
veal, or lamb, served in pitta bread to take away).

Crete is often celebrated for its *stiffádo* (braised beef with
onions). In country villages you'll also find traditional *katzíka*
(goat meat dishes served in tomato sauce). *Brizoles* (grilled
steak) usually comes well done unless you specify otherwise.
Also try *keftédes* (spicy lamb meat balls), *kokorétsi* (spiced
sausages of innards and herbs), or *kotópoulo* (roasted chicken).

Yoghurt and Cheese

Thick, creamy Greek yoghurt, topped with Cretan thyme
honey (*méli*) or fresh fruit, is one of the most scrumptious

treats on the island. It makes a great breakfast, café snack or refreshing take-away from the *galaktopolío* (dairy counter).

Cheeses are generally made out of sheep's or goat's milk.

> **Vegetables are usually eaten cold (raw or boiled, and then cooled), or tepid.**

Féta is the well-known soft cheese served on Greek salads—it is delicious fried as a starter. Crete's *anthótyro* and *manoúri* are relatively bland, *graviéera* is harder and sharper. Other hard cheeses include the *agrafáou* and the salty *kefalotíri*. A rare blue cheese to hold its own against any French variety is *kopanistí*.

Dessert

The Greeks eat their dessert at the *zacharoplastío* (pastry shop) on the way home. Tavernas seldom have a full selection. Among the most popular desserts (all containing lots of honey) are: *baklavá* (a honey-drenched flaky pastry with walnuts and almonds), *loukoúm* (a doughnut-like honey fritter), *kataífi* (shredded wheat filled with honey or syrup and chopped almonds), and *pítta me méli* (honey cake). Evidently of Venetian inspiration, *rizógalo* is a creamy-smooth rice pudding. *Galaktoboúriko* is a custard pie.

DRINKS

Coffee

Happily, filter coffee and cappuccino have found their way on to the island, a welcome alternative to the all-too-common instant variety (called

Beach tavernas offer many delicious Greek specialities.

nes or *neskafé*) usually served to foreigners. If you want coffee with milk, you should ask for *kafé me gála*.

Traditional Greek coffee (*ellinikó*) is thick and strong, boiled to order in a long-handled copper or aluminium pot and poured, grounds and all, into a tiny cup. It is served with a glass of cold water. To be certain of getting it freshly brewed to your liking, ask for *éna vari glikó* (heavy and sweet), *glykí vastró* (sweet but boiled thinner), *éna métrio* (medium-sweet), or *éna skéto* (without sugar).

Wine, Beer and Spirits

Cretan wines, once highly regarded in the ancient world, can be very good and go well with the local cuisine. It's worth trying the white wines (*áspro*) of Olympia, Minos, Logado, Górtis, and Lató. The reds (*mávro*—"black") tend to be full-bodied and rich in alcohol. The best local reds come from Sitía. Archanes is another excellent wine region. Kissamos, Mantiko, and Armanti reds are also good bets. You'll find that house wines served in a carafe are usually dark rosé (*kókkino*).

> Greek coffee: the beans are ground to a fine powder, boiled with water, and then poured, grounds and all, into a cup. Let the grounds settle then drink just half the cup.

Retsina, the pine-resinated white wine that is so popular on the mainland, is now produced on Crete. It takes but a short time to acquire the taste and discover how well it goes with both seafood and lamb. But if you really don't like it, it is possible to specify *aretsinoto* (unresinated wine) when ordering.

Although there are no Greek beers, good European brands are brewed locally under licence from parent companies, and are inexpensive.

Rakí, also called *tsikoudiá*, is the strong local firewater, tasting somewhat like Italian *grappa*. It's traditionally offered as a sign of hospitality. Strongest of the lot is Réthimnon's *mournorakí*, made out of mulberries.

The aniseed-flavoured *oúzo*, served neat or with ice and water, is popular on Crete, as is the Greek brandy *Metaxa*, in grades of 3, 5, or 7 stars. You might also like to try Crete's sweet dessert wine, *Malevízi*, or the tangerine liqueur known as *mandaríni*.

To Help You Order...

Could we have a table?	**Tha boroúsame na échoume éna trapézi?**
I'd like a/an/some…	**Tha íthela…**
beer	**mía bíra**
bread	**psomí**
coffee	**éna kafé**
cutlery	**macheropírouna**
dessert	**éna glíko**
fish	**psári**
fruit	**froúta**
glass	**éna potíri**
ice cream	**éna pagotó**
meat	**kréas**
milk	**gála**
mineral water	**metallikó neró**
rice	**rízi**
salad	**mía saláta**
soup	**mía soúpa**
sugar	**záchari**
table napkin	**éna trapezo mándilo**
tea	**éna tsaï**
(iced) water	**(pagoméno) neró**
wine	**krasí**

INDEX

HANDY TRAVEL TIPS

An A–Z Summary of Practical Information

A

ACCOMMODATION *(ΔΩMATIA—domátia)*

(See also Camping on page 103, Youth Hostels on page 128, and Recommended Hotels starting on page 129).

Offices of the Greek National Tourist Organization (signposted EOT) and most good travel agents have a list of hotels by price and category. Many of the larger hotels are often fully booked for the high season by package tour operators abroad, but if you do arrive without a reservation a room will usually be found for you somewhere. If your boat or charter flight arrives in the early hours, ask a taxi driver to help you find a hotel.

Hotel prices are government-controlled, based on the building's age, facilities and other factors. Hotels are rated from A to E, but this only establishes minimum rates and prices can vary widely within each band according to the season, location, and availability of rooms. Luxury establishments (L) are not price-controlled.

Categories C and above all have private bathrooms. In lower categories, rooms with bath are rare, though almost all rooms have showers. Rates and all extra charges (such as air-conditioning, television, or hot water if your room has no private facilities) must by law be posted in your hotel room. During high season some hotels require that you take half board (lunch or dinner). Check in advance to avoid surprises with the bill. Price reductions are often offered for children.

Rooms. In the main resorts, rooms are generally purpose-built in modern blocks, but in country villages away from the coast you can find pleasant rooms in Cretan homes, often with bath or shower or cooking facilities. Look for the "Rent Room" sign (in English, or often "zimmer frei" or "chambre a louer").

Villas. Self-catering accommodation ranges from small, simple cottages to quite lavish summer houses or well-equipped apartments, let on a monthly or even weekly basis. When booking, ascertain the complete facilities, which normally (but not always) include refrigerator, hot water and electricity.

When arranging for a villa from abroad, be sure to inquire about accessibility to food shops and nearby beaches if you are going to be without transport.

Crete

I'd like a single/double room.	**Tha íthela éna monó/dipló domátio.**
with bath/shower	**me bánio/dous**
What is the rate per night?	**Piá íne i timí giá mía níkta?**

AIRPORTS (ΑΕΡΟΔΡΟΜΙΟ—*aerodrómio*)

Crete has two main airports. Almost all international flights come into Iráklion, 3 km (2 miles) east of the capital. Some charter flights-from abroad, as well as flights from Athens, also arrive at Chaniá, 15 km (9½ miles) from town. Sitía's airport deals with domestic flights only. Olympic Airways is the Greek airline for international and domestic flights, with offices in all of the main towns and resorts.

Iráklion airport has recently been renovated and expanded. It offers a range of car rental firms and travel agency counters as well as the usual amenities of restaurant, snack-bar and duty-free shop. There is a currency exchange office, which is usually open to meet international flights arriving at night. However, it is a good idea to buy Greek currency before travelling just in case it is closed. Trolleys are available for a small charge.

Taxis are plentiful in addition to public airport bus services, to take you into town. Taxi rates to outlying resorts and towns are posted in the arrivals area.

For airport information, tel. (081) 228402 (Iráklion); tel. (0821) 63224 (Chaniá). For lost property at Iráklion airport, call Olympic Airways, tel. (081) 245644, ext. 209.

Where's the bus for…?	**Pou íne to leoforío giá…?**
Taxi!	**Taxí!**

B

BICYCLE and MOTORSCOOTER RENTAL (ΕΝΟΙΚΙΑΣΕΙΣ ΠΟΔΗΛΑΤΩΝ/ΜΟΤΟΠΟΔΗΛΑΤΩΝ—*enikIásis podiláton/ motopodiláton*) (See also Planning Your Budget on page 119)

This is a thriving business in all the resort towns. During high season, reserve early on busy Sundays and public holidays. Make sure the price includes proper insurance. Motor scooters are best used in town and on flat coastal roads—the interior is too hilly for anything but a motorbike.

Very few people wear helmets as they can be uncomfortable in the heat of the summer, but remember that accidents are common, especially on Crete's busy and winding roads. If you rent a motorcycle, insist on a crash helmet—it's against the law to ride without one. Inspect brakes, tyres, etc., before hiring, and drive with care.

What's the rental charge for a full day? **Póso kostízi giá mía iméra?**

C

CAMPING (ΚΑΜΠΙΝΓΚ— *"camping"*)
(See also Tourist Information Offices on page 124)

Only official campsites may be used. There are 17 of them open from May to September—a complete list with telephone numbers is available from the Greek National Tourist Office. The most popular are those near Hersónissos on the north coast, and at Ierápetra, Mátala, Agía Galíni, and Paleochóra on the south coast.

Is there a campsite nearby? **Ipárchi éna méros giá "camping" edó kondá?**

May we camp here? **Boroúme na kataskinósoume edó?**

Can I hire/buy a sleeping bag? **Boró na nikiáso/agoráso éna "sleeping bag"?**

CAR RENTAL
(ΕΝΟΙΚΙΑΣΕΙΣ ΑΦΤΟΚΙΝΗΤΟΝ—*enikiásis aftokiníton*)
(See Driving on page 109 and Planning Your Budget on page 119)

There are plenty of car rental firms on Crete, but it's not cheap to hire a car. Local companies offer increasingly competitive prices compared with the fixed rates of the major international rental firms, especially off season. However, if you're booking in advance from home, the big firms are the best bet in high season if you want to be sure of a car, as the number of vehicles available from local companies may be limited at your resort.

Locally, it is wiser to rent your car with a credit card than have to haggle over the amount of reimbursement from a cash deposit. Deposits are often waived for credit card holders and members of large tour groups, who may also obtain a small discount.

Make sure you clarify what is and is not included in the quoted price, especially as regards insurance. Third-party liability insurance should be included in the rate, but not all companies give full accidental damage coverage in their inclusive rates. Complete coverage is usually available for a modest extra charge. Remember that insurance does not cover any damage to tyres or the underside of the car, and sometimes the windscreen, if you take the car on very rough roads. Enquire whether mileage is included or is charged in addition. All rates are subject to a stamp duty and local taxes. Most firms take credit cards, but you may be asked to pay cash if you are getting a discounted rate.

Agencies require a valid driving licence that has been held for at least one year. Non-EU licences may also require an International Driving Permit. Depending on the model and the hiring firm, minimum age for renting a car varies from 21 to 25.

I'd like to rent a car (tomorrow).	**Tha íthela na nikiáso éna aftokínito (ávrio).**
for one day/a week	**giá mía iméra/mía evdomáda**
Please include full insurance.	**Sas parakaló na simberilávete miktí asfália.**

CLIMATE and CLOTHING

Crete has a good climate throughout the year and the south coast stays warm right through the winter. Even in the coolest months of January and February, the temperature seldom drops below 8ºC (46ºF). Spring is short, but beautifully green and the countryside is bursting with wild flowers; there is some rain in April. Mountain peaks are snowcapped until June. Summers are baking hot; the strong *méltemi* wind alleviates some of the heat, but can make the seas rough and the sand beaches unpleasant. Autumn is cooler and less crowded, though the nights and the seas can be chilly and there is some rain in October. Many resorts and hotels close from November until Easter. If you come in the colder months (November-April), note that smaller hotels may not have heating. The mountain ranges also affect the climate throughout the year, and if there is bad weather on the north coast, the south coast is often sunny and fine.

Approximate monthly average temperatures (Iráklion):

		J	F	M	A	M	J	J	A	S	O	N	D
Air (max.)	°C	16	16	18	21	24	28	30	39	28	26	21	19
	°F	60	60	64	70	76	82	86	86	82	78	70	66
Air (min.)	°C	9	9	10	12	16	18	20	22	20	17	14	11
	°F	48	48	50	54	60	64	68	72	68	62	57	52
Sea temp.	°C	16	16	17	18	20	23	24	25	24	23	19	17
	°F	61	61	63	64	68	73	75	77	75	73	66	63

Clothing (*rouchismós*) is almost always casual on Crete. A tie is practically never expected, even in the smartest restaurant, and a jacket only rarely. However, many hotel dining rooms discourage shorts in the evening. Similarly, put on a shirt or sarong for the trip to or from the beach. When visiting churches or monasteries, women are expected to dress modestly, and no one should wear shorts.

Bring a sweater or light jacket, even for summer evenings, especially for trips up into the mountains, and light rainwear for visits in the spring or autumn. A hat and sunglasses are recommended, especially in summer. Good sandals or "thongs" can be bought on the island to protect against the hot sand or rocks. One absolute must: sturdy, comfortable shoes for visits to archaeological sites, and caves and hiking in the mountains, particularly the Samariá Gorge.

Is it all right if I wear this?   **Tha íme endáxi an foréso aftó?**

COMMUNICATIONS

Post Office (ΤΑΧΥΔΡΟΜΕΙΟ—*tachidromío*). The post offices handle letters, stamp sales, parcels, money orders, and currency exchange, but not telegrams and phone calls (which are handled by offices of the Greek phone company, OTE). Post offices can be recognized by a yellow sign (the same colour as the letter boxes) marked with the letters ΕΛΤΑ. Most places that sell postcards also sell stamps, usually at a small surcharge.

In Ágios Nikólaos, the post office is located on 28 Octovriou Street; in Chaniá at 3 Tzanakáki Street; in Iráklion on Platía Daskaloyiánnis (main office) and at El Greco Park (substation); in Réthimnon on Koundourioti (main office), and by the beach on S. Venizélou (substation).

Crete

Registered letters and parcels going out of Greece are checked at the post office desk before being sent, so don't seal them beforehand. Express special delivery service exists for an extra charge.

Local post offices are open 7:30 or 8am-2pm, Monday to Friday. In the major towns they are often open until 8pm and on weekends as well. In tourist hotels, the receptionist will usually dispatch mail.

General delivery/poste restante. If you don't know your address ahead of time, you can have your mail sent poste restante, with your surname in capital letters and underlined, and marked *poste restante*, to the main post office of the town where you'll be staying. It will be held for a month, and you will need your passport for identification when collecting mail.

Telephones, telegrams and **fax** (*tiléfono*; *tilegráfima*). Each major town on Crete has an office of Greece's telecommunications organization (OTE), open daily 7am-midnight. Those in the smaller towns have shorter hours (usually 7:30am-10pm, Monday to Friday). Here you can send telegrams and dial direct, both locally and abroad, in metered cubicles, or have an operator obtain the number for you. There are also fax services.

International trunk lines are often busy and you may have to wait up to two hours at peak times. This is especially true for reverse-charge (collect) calls.

You can also make international calls from many coin- or card-operated phone booths around the island. Coin phones accept 10-, 20-, and 50-drachma coins, and phone cards starting at 100 units can be bought at kiosks and OTE offices. Avoid making long-distance calls from your hotel, as some add a 50% surcharge. Phoning from street kiosks is also pricy, and they have terrible overseas connections.

Long-distance calls become less expensive after 8pm and after 10pm on Sundays.

To call overseas dial "00" followed by the code for the country you are calling (see list below), then the area code, leaving off the initial "0," then the number itself.

UK	00 44
USA	00 1
Canada	00 1
Australia	00 61

New Zealand   **00 64**

South Africa   **00 27**

Dial **161** to get an international operator, **151** for operator and **131** for local directory enquiries.

The area codes for the main towns on Crete are:

Iráklion 081	**Chaniá** 0821	**Réthimnon** 0831
Ágios Nikólaos 0841	**Sitía** 0843	**Ierápetra** 0842

Where's the nearest post office?	**Pou íne to kodinótero tachidromío?**
Have you received any mail for…?	**Échete grámmata giá…?**
A stamp for this letter/ postcard, please.	**Éna grammatósimo giaftó to grámma/kart postál, parakaló.**
express (special delivery)	**exprés**
airmail	**aeroporikós**
registered	**sistiméno**
I want to send a telegram to…	**Thélo na stilo éna tilegráfima sto…**
Can you get this number in…?	**Boríte na mou párete aftó ton arithmó…?**
reverse-charge (collect) call	**plirotéo apó to paralípti**
person-to-person (personal) call	**prosopikí klísi**

COMPLAINTS *(See also Police on page 122)*

If you really feel you have been cheated or misled, raise the matter first with the manager or proprietor of the establishment in question. If you still do not get satisfaction, take the problem to the Tourist Police, tel. 171. All hotels and public places of amusement are price-controlled by the government. If it can be proved that you have been overcharged, the matter will be settled quickly. Often, just mentioning the words "tourist police" will get results—and remember that complaints made with a smile are much more effective than angry glares or shouting.

CRIME *(See also Emergencies on page 112)*

Crime is relatively rare on Crete compared with other holiday destinations. Honesty is a matter of pride among Cretans—if you leave something in a shop or restaurant, the proprietor will do his or her

Crete

best to find it. However, take common sense precautions such as depositing valuables in your hotel safe and watching your handbag in public. Take particular care of your passport.

Possession of drugs is a serious matter in Greece. Make sure you have a prescription from your doctor if you'll be carrying syringes, insulin, any narcotic drugs or codeine, which is illegal in Greece.

CUSTOMS and ENTRY FORMALITIES

Visitors from European Union (EU) countries need only an identity card (or U.K. passport) to enter Greece. Citizens of most other countries must be in possession of a valid passport. European and North American residents are not subject to any health requirements. In case of doubt, check with the Greek representatives in your own country before your departure.

Duty-free allowance. As Greece is part of the **European Union**, free exchange of non-duty-free goods for personal use is permitted between Crete and the UK and the Republic of Ireland. However, duty-free items are still subject to restrictions, so check before you go. Current limits are 200 cigarettes **or** 50 cigars **or** 250g tobacco; 2*l* table wine **and** 1*l* spirits **or** 2*l* fortified or sparkling wine **or** liqueurs **or** a further 2*l* of still wine; 50g (60cc or 2fl oz) perfume **or** 250g toilet water; £71 worth of other goods.

Non-EU country residents returning home may bring back the following duty-free amounts:

Into:	Cigarettes		Cigars		Tobacco	Spirits		Wine
Australia:	250	or			250g	1*l*	or	1*l*
Canada:	200	and	50	and	400g	1.14*l*	or	8.5*l*
New Zealand:	200	or	50	or	250g	1.1*l*	or	4.5*l*
South Africa:	400	and	50	and	250g	1*l*	and	2*l*
USA:	200	and	100	and	2kg	1*l*	or	1*l*

Medicines. Certain prescription drugs, including tranquillizers and headache preparations, cannot be carried into the country without a prescription or official medical document. Fines—even jail sentences—have been imposed on the unwary tourist.

Currency restrictions. Non-residents may import up to 100,000drs and export up to 20,000drs (in denominations no larger than 5,000drs). There is no limit on the foreign currency or traveller's cheques you may import or export as a tourist, though any amount in excess of US$1,000 or its equivalent should be declared to the customs official upon arrival if you intend to take it out again.

Antiquities (*archéa*). Most antiquities may be exported only with the approval of the Greek Archaeological Service (which is in Athens), and after paying a fee. Anyone caught smuggling out an artefact may receive a long prison sentence and a stiff fine, and the item will be confiscated. Beachcombers should not even think of using a metal-detector—this is totally illegal. If you do stumble upon an ancient amphora or are offered a "genuine Byzantine icon," contact the head of the local museum, *before* handing over any money, to find out if you may take it home with you. Travellers purchasing an antiquity should get the dealer to obtain an export permit.

I have nothing to declare.	**Den écho na dilóso típota.**
It's for my personal use.	**Íne giá prosopikí chrísi.**

D

DRIVING IN CRETE *(See also Car Rental on page 103)*

Entering Greece. To bring your car into Greece you'll need car registration papers, nationality plate or sticker, a valid driving licence and insurance coverage (the Green Card is no longer compulsory within the EU, although comprehensive coverage is advisable). Contact the Association of Insurance Companies in Athens at (01) 323-6733 for specific information about coverage in Greece.

Normally, you may drive a car in Greece for up to four months on your ordinary licence, provided it has been held for one year. An international driving licence (not required for holders of a British licence) is obtainable through your home motoring association.

Driving regulations. The standard European red warning triangle is required in Greece for emergencies. Despite the laxness you may observe on the island, seat belts are obligatory, as are crash helmets for motorcycle drivers and their passengers. The police can suddenly clamp down and fines for non-compliance are high.

Drive on the right and pass on the left. Many local drivers have a bad habit of not always returning to the near-side lane, and of passing on right or left indiscriminately. Traffic from the right has right of way. Note that if a driver flashes lights, it means "Stay where you are," not "Go ahead."

Driving conditions on Crete. The National Highway, which extends along the north coast and connects all the major towns, is for almost its entire length broad and well maintained. (note, though, that slow-moving traffic is often forced into the shoulder while faster cars use the regular lane for passing). At the eastern end beyond Ágios Nikólaos, the scenery and hairpin bends make equal demands on your attention. Many Cretans drive well above the posted 80 km/h (50 mph) on this road. They use the shoulder as an unofficial slow lane and expect you to do the same, which can be unnerving on blind curves.

Expect to encounter impatience—flashing lights, beeping horns, passing on blind curves, and all manner of road manoeuvres that range from simply rude to downright suicidal. Drive defensively! Many drivers seldom use their rear view mirrors and expect you to honk when overtaking.

Both main highways and secondary roads are usually asphalted and in good condition, but it is folly to drive at high speeds on this mountainous island. Most roads are steep and winding, curves are often sharp and sudden; if you see a sign to reduce speed, slow down promptly. Rock-fall along the shoulders is common—and dangerous—particularly in the rainy season. Watch out for sheep and other animals, cyclists and locals who are in no hurry to get out of the way, but do not expect Cretan drivers to return the compliment when *you* are the pedestrian!

Road signs on main roads and at junctions appear generally in both Greek and Roman letters; off the beaten track they may be in Greek only.

Traffic police. Patrol cars have the word Police in large letters on the doors. They are particularly severe on speeding and illegal parking and may give you a cash fine.

Petrol. You can get normal-grade petrol (90-octane), super (98), lead-free and diesel. Service stations are plentiful on the island, but check your fuel gauge before heading for the more remote areas.

Breakdowns and accidents. Your car hire firm should give you a number to call in case of a breakdown or accident. For road assistance you can also contact the Automobile Association of Greece (ELPA), tel. **104** (emergencies) or **174** (information).

Fluid measures

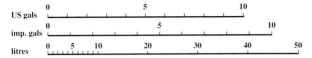

Distance

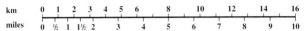

Road signs. Most road signs are the standard pictographs used throughout Europe, and most are written in both Greek and Roman lettering. However, you may encounter the following signs in Greek:

ΑΔΙΕΞΟΔΟΣ	No through road
ΑΛΤ/ΣΤΟΜ	Stop
ΑΝΩΜΑΛΙΑ ΟΔΟΣΤΡΩΜΑΤΟΣ	Bad road surface
ΑΠΑΓΟΡΕΥΕΤΑΙ Η ΕΙΣΟΔΟΣ	No entry
ΑΠΑΓΟΡΕΥΕΤΑΙ Η ΣΤΑΘΜΕΥΣΙΣ	No parking
ΚΙΝΔΥΝΟΣ	Caution
ΜΟΝΟΔΡΟΜΟΣ	One-way traffic
ΠΑΡΑΚΑΜΠΤΗΡΙΟΣ	Diversion (detour)

Are we on the right road for…?	**Ímaste sto sostó drómo giá…?**
Full tank, please.	**Na to gemísete me venzíni.**
normal/super/lead-free	**aplí/soúper/amólivdos**
My car has broken down.	**Épatha mía vlávi.**

E

ELECTRICITY

Greece has 220-volt, 50-cycle AC current. Sockets are either two- or three-pin. Hotels are seldom able to supply plug adaptors, so it's best to bring one from home.

I need an adaptor/a battery.	**Chriázome énas metaschimatistís/ mía bataria.**

Crete

EMBASSIES and CONSULATES *(presvía; proxenío)*

British consulate (also for citizens of Ireland and Commonwealth countries not separately represented): Papalexándrou Square 16, Iráklion; tel. (081) 224012. Emergency telephone (British embassy, Athens): tel. (01) 723-6211.

Embassies of all major countries are located in Athens.

Australia: Odós Soutsou 37, 115-21 Athens; tel. (01) 644-7303.

Canada: Ioannou Genedíou 1, 115-21 Athens; tel. (01) 725-4011.

Ireland: Leofóros Vas. Konstantínou 7, 106-74 Athens; tel. (01) 723-2771.

New Zealand: Semitelou 9, 115-28 Athens; tel. (01) 771-0112.

South Africa: Leofóros Kifissías 60, 151-25 Athens; tel. (01) 680-6645.

UK: Ploutárchou 1, 106-75 Athens; tel. (01) 723-6211.

U.S.A.: Leofóros Vas. Sofías 91, 115-21 Athens; tel. (01) 721-2951.

EMERGENCIES *(See also Medical Care on page 117 and Police on page 122)*

Except in more remote areas, you will usually find someone who speaks English who will be able to help you. If you are alone and near a telephone, here are some important numbers:

Police/Emergencies	**100**
Ambulance	**166**
Fire	**199**
Road assistance	**104, 174**
Tourist Police	**171**

Though we hope you'll never need them, here are a few words you may like to learn in advance:

Careful	**Prosochí**
Fire	**Fotiá**
Help	**Voíthia**
Police	**Astinomía**
Stop thief!	**Stamatíste to kléfti**

ENVIRONMENTAL ISSUES

Though you may be tempted to buy exotic souvenirs, spare a thought for endangered animals and plants that may be threatened by your purchase. Over 800 species of animals and plants are currently banned from international trade and a further 23,000 are controlled by CITES (Convention on International Trade in Endangered Species and Plants). These include many corals, shells, cacti, ,and hardwoods as well as the more obvious tigers, rhinos, spotted cats, and turtles.

ETIQUETTE

Cretan hospitality remains, by and large, sincere and generous. Even if you have been brought up to believe that it is polite to start by saying "No, thank you" to unexpected offers of hospitality, you may find you hurt the feelings of your would-be host here by responding in such a way. If you are ever taken aback, do let your surprise be clearly appreciative.

From the humblest ceramics shop to the most elegant jewellers, you may be offered a cup of coffee. Accepting this friendly gesture does not carry with it an obligation to buy. In a Cretan home, particularly in a country village, you will be plied with food and drink—don't feel ill at ease if you alone are served while your hostess looks on; it is a traditional expression of hospitality.

Staring is not considered rude in Greece. On the contrary, it is a flattering sign of interest in you, satisfying a characteristic curiosity, and means no harm at all. In the same spirit, it is usual to ask personal questions about your family, your home, your work.

Like the Spanish *mañana*, the Greek *ávrio* is more vague than tomorrow—at best, "soon." Learn to take your time and smile.

Greeks, in common with most continental Europeans, wish each other "bon appetit" before starting a meal. In Greek, the expression is *kalí órexi*! A common toast when drinking is *stin igiá* (*"ya"*) *sas*! meaning "cheers!" A reply to any toast, in the sense of "the same to you," is *epísis*.

The simple courtesies mean a lot in Greece and not only win friends, but help smooth your own way.

G

GAY and LESBIAN TRAVELLERS

There are no resorts on Crete specifically geared to gay travellers. Attitudes are generally relaxed, though discretion is also appreciated in this traditional Orthodox country. Homosexuality is legal in Greece over the age of 17.

GUIDES and TOURS *(xenagós; periodía)*
(See also Tourist Information Offices on page 124)

The local tourist office can refer you to an officially recognized guide for visiting historic sites or to accompany you on a hike in the mountains. You could also enlist a taxi driver who speaks good English and knows the sights, but arrange a price beforehand.

You will also be approached by guides at entrances to many of the main sites; they are not obligatory, but if you use them agree a price in advance. Occasionally locals will approach you and offer to show you something of interest, such as an old building behind a gate, but don't feel obligated if they then ask you for money.

Travel agencies abound all over the island. They offer tours to the main archaeological sites and scenic areas, popular beaches, the Samariá and Imbros gorges, as well as day trips and cruises to Santorini and several offshore islands.

We'd like an English-speaking guide.	**Tha thélame éna xenagó na milái in angliká.**
I need an English interpreter.	**Chriázome ánglo diermenéa.**
How much?	**Póso káni?**

L

LANGUAGE *(See also Useful Expressions on the cover of this guide)*

Most people in contact with foreign visitors on Crete speak a certain amount of English and/or German, and often some French or Italian as well. Restaurant menus are printed in several languages, as are tourist brochures.

Stress is a very important feature of the Greek language and is indicated in our transcription throughout this guide by an accent mark (´) above the vowel of the syllable to be emphasized.

The table below lists the Greek letters in their capital and small forms, followed by the letters to which they correspond in English.

A	α	a	as in b**a**r
B	β	v	
Γ	γ	g	as in **g**o*
Δ	δ	d	like **th** in **th**is
E	ε	e	as in g**e**t
Z	ζ	z	
H	η	h	like **ee** in m**ee**t
Θ	θ	th	as in **th**in
I	ι	i	like **ee** in m**ee**t
K	κ	k	
Λ	λ	l	
M	μ	m	
N	ν	n	
Ξ	ξ	x	like **ks** in than**ks**
O	ο	o	as in g**o**t
Π	π	p	
P	ρ	r	
Σ	σ, ς	s	as in ki**ss**
T	τ	t	
Y	υ	i	like **ee** in m**ee**t
Φ	φ	f	
X	χ	ch	as in Scottish lo**ch**
Ψ	ψ	ps	as in ti**ps**y
<u>O</u>/Ω	ω	o	as in g**o**t
OY	ου	oo	as in s**ou**p

*except before **i**- and **e**- sounds, when it's pronounced like **y** in **y**es.

You'll find a list of useful expressions on the cover of this guide, and the *Berlitz Greek Phrase Book and Dictionary* covers practically all situations you're likely to encounter in your travels.

Crete

LAUNDRY and DRY-CLEANING

(ΠΛΥΝΤΗΡΙΟ—*plintírio*; ΚΑΘΑΡΙΣΤΗΡΙΟ—*katharistírio*)

In this climate it's easy to rinse out small articles yourself. They will dry in just a few hours.

During the peak season, allow three or four days for hotel laundry and dry-cleaning services (two days the rest of the year). Same-day service costs extra. Local laundry services are adequate but can be tough on delicate colours. There are laundrettes in the larger towns.

Where's the nearest laundry/ dry cleaners?	**Pou íne to kodinótero plintírio/katharistírio?**
When will it be ready?	**Póte tha íne étimo?**

LOST PROPERTY (*See also Embassies and Consulates on page 112 and Police on page 122*)

Given the general level of honesty among Cretans, the chances of re-covering lost property are good. If you have problems, call the tourist police. Should you lose your passport, report it to the police and contact your consulate in Athens. It's wise to keep a note of your traveller's cheque serial numbers, passport and other document details.

I've lost my wallet/ handbag/passport.	**Échasa to portofóli mou/ti tsánda mou/ to diavatirió mou.**

M

MEDIA

Radio and television (*rádio*; *tileórasi*). Local Greek radio and TV broadcast news in English daily, and there are French and German broadcasts on ET1. For transmission times, consult the local English-language newspaper. With a transistor radio you can also pick up the BBC World Service and Voice of America quite clearly in the evening and early morning.

Almost all hotels on the island have television lounges, as do many tavernas and restaurants. English-language series and films are run in the original version with Greek subtitles. Some of the bigger hotels show English-language video films or have satellite TV.

Newspapers, magazines, books (*efimerída*; *periodikó*; *vivlío*). The principal British newspapers, the *International Herald Tribune*, and other foreign dailies and magazines are on sale at shops and kiosks throughout the island. During the summer, free newspapers are published for tourists at the main resorts, advertising events, restaurants, etc. Look for *This Month Crete*, a bilingual English-German publication that includes feature articles. The English-language *Athens News* carries Greek and international news.

For a wide range of novels, classics, guidebooks, maps and non-fiction books in several languages, try Planet Bookstore, Hortatsou, and Kidonías streets in Iráklion (tel. 081/281558); International Press, 81 El. Venizélou in Réthimnon (tel. 0831/24111); and the bookshops on Hálidon Street in Chaniá.

Have you any English-language newspapers? **Échete anglikés efimerídes?**

MEDICAL CARE *(See also Customs and Entry Formalities on page 108 and Emergencies on page 112)*

European Union citizens with an E111 form (obtainable in their own country) can have free treatment under the Greek health service. However, it's advisable to take out private holiday insurance as well to cover accidents and illness—hospital facilities may be over-stretched in the tourist season and you will generally get better medical care if you have insurance. Vaccinations are not necessary before you go to Crete. Note that there are strict regulations on the carrying of prescription drugs into the country.

If required, your hotel should be able to find you a doctor or dentist who speaks English. Most resorts have a local surgery, with hours and telephone numbers posted.

In an **emergency**, dial **166** for ambulance dispatch (24-hour).

Hospital numbers for the major towns are:

Iráklion: (081) 237502

Chaniá: (0821) 27231

Réthimnon: (0831) 27814

Ágios Nikólaos: (0841) 25221

The two main health hazards are sunburn and minor stomach upsets, so take food, drink, and sun in moderation. Use a high-factor sun cream, avoid the midday sun, and wear a hat and sunglasses.

Crete

To combat mosquito attacks, bring along mosquito repellent. You can also buy inflammable coils called *katól*, or a small electric device that you plug in at night, to keep the bugs at bay (available on Crete).

If you step on a sea urchin, apply lemon juice or olive oil—some suggest a well mixed dressing of both! A jellyfish sting can be relieved by ammonia, but in case of severe swelling, see a doctor.

Pharmacies (ΦAPMAKEIO—*farmakío*). A red or green cross on a white background identifies a pharmacy (chemist). They keep normal shop opening hours, but there is at least one on 24-hour duty, on a rotating basis, in each major town. Pharmacies display details of night and weekend services. Your hotel, tour guide, or the tourist police will also help you locate the right one.

Without a prescription, you won't be able to obtain sleeping pills, barbiturates or medicine for stomach upsets. Condoms are also available at city kiosks and sometimes at dispensing machines outside the pharmacies in some resorts.

Where's the nearest (all-night) pharmacy?	**Pou íne to kodinótero (dianikterévon) farmakío?**
a doctor/a dentist	**énas giatrós/énas odontogiatrós**
an ambulance	**éna asthenofóro**
hospital	**nosokomío**
an upset stomach	**varistomachiá**
sunstroke	**ilíasi**

MONEY MATTERS

Currency (*nómisma*). Greece's monetary unit is the drachma (*drachmi*, abbreviated "drs"—in Greek, ΔΡΑΧΜΕΣ).
Coins: 1, 2, 5, 10, 20, 50, 100drs.
Banknotes: 50, 100, 500, 1,000, 5,000drs.

Banks and currency exchange (ΤΡΑΠΕΖΑ∇*trápeza*; ΣΥΝΑΛ–ΛΑΓΜΑ—*sinállagma*). Major banks have branches in all the main towns and resorts. In the smaller resorts you will have to rely on travel agencies for currency exchange. You will usually get a better exchange rate at the banks, but there is frequently a long wait at their counters. Some travel agents and hotels offer bank rates, and you may prefer paying their commission (2% is common) as a fee for the convenience. Main post offices also provide currency exchange facilities, as do many historical sites, restaurants and shops.

Credit cards (*pistotikí kárta*). Internationally known credit cards are honoured in many shops catering to tourists and by banks, car rental firms, and leading hotels. You can also use the cashpoint machines outside main banks, which accept major cards; instructions are given in several languages.

Traveller's cheques. Most major brands of traveller's cheques, in any western currency, are readily cashed. Always take your passport for identification. Eurocheques are now accepted in many places.

I want to change some pounds/dollars.	**Thélo na merikés líres/meriká dollária.**
Do you accept traveller's cheques?	**Pérnete "traveller's cheques'?**
Can I pay with this credit card?	**Boró na pliróso ma aftí ti pistotikí kárta?**
Have you something cheaper?	**Échete káti ftinótero?**

PLANNING YOUR BUDGET

Opposite are some average prices in Greek drachmas. Owing to inflation and the fact that prices rise with each new tourist season, they can only be regarded as approximate.

Airport transfer. *Iráklion*: taxi 1,200drs to town centre. *Chaniá*: taxi 2,500drs to town centre.

Babysitters. 1,500-2,000drs per hour.

Bicycle and motorscooter rental. *Mountain bikes* 3,900drs per day, 19,900drs per week. *Motorscooters* from 4,500drs per day, 19,500drs per week.

Camping (average prices per day). 950drs per adult, tents 600-800drs, cars 500-700drs, caravans (trailers) 1,000drs.

Car rental (international company, high season, booking on Crete). Class A, e.g. *Fiat Panda*: 15,500drs per day or 90,000drs per week. Class B, e.g. *Opel Corsa*: 18,000drs per day, 100,000drs per week. Prices include unlimited mileage, collision damage waiver and 18% tax. Advance reservations from home or local companies may be less expensive; rates are often negotiable, especially off-season. Many companies add a rate per km for short-term rentals.

Cigarettes. Greek brands 350-450drs per packet of 20; foreign brands 500-750drs.

Entertainment. *Bouzoúki* music evening including food, 5,000drs and up; disco from 1,000drs; cinema 1,500drs.

Hotels (double room with bath, during the summer season). Luxury from 30,000drs. Class A from 18,000drs. Class B 10,000-14,000drs. Class C 7,000-10,000drs. Class D 6,000-7,000drs.

Meals and drinks. Breakfast 800-2,000drs. Lunch or dinner in fairly good establishment 2,000-5,000drs. Coffee (instant) 400drs, *oúzo* with *mezédes* 450drs, Greek brandy 500drs, gin and tonic 600drs, beer 400drs, wine 400drs, soft drinks 300drs.

Museums. Adults 800-1,500drs, children and seniors 250-750drs.

Sports. *Sunbeds and beach umbrellas* 500-700drs each. *Yacht* from 23,500drs per day. *Pedalo/canoe* 2,500/1,500drs per hour. *Water-skiing* 3,000drs for 1 circuit (10 minutes). *Parasailing* 6,500drs 1 person, 9,500drs 2 persons. *Windsurfing* 3,500drs per hour. *Tennis* from 2,000drs per person per hour.

O

OPENING HOURS *(See also Public Holidays on page 122)*

Banks. Banks are open 8am-2pm Monday to Thursday, to 1:30pm on Friday. In summer at least one bank remains open in larger towns 5-7pm and for short periods on Saturdays for money changing only.

Shops. Shops are generally open 8am-2:30pm Monday to Saturday, and again in the evenings 5-8pm on Tuesdays, Thursdays, and Fridays. Most shops are closed on Sundays. In high season, shops and supermarkets catering for tourists in resort areas stay open throughout the day and on Sundays.

Siesta. With the exception of a few tourist-geared shops, everything starts closing down at 1:30pm and opens again around 4 or 5pm. Noise is very much frowned upon between these hours. Work resumes again after the siesta until around 8 or 9pm.

Museums and historical sites. Hours vary from year to year and town to town, so check with the local tourist information office. Most museums and archaeological sites are open 8:30am-3pm; the major ones stay open until 6pm. Many museums and sites are free on Sundays. Most close one day a week, usually Monday, and may be closed on some national holidays.

Churches. In main towns, churches are open in the morning until around 1pm and again in the evening.

Post Offices. In the main towns post offices are open 7:30 or 8am-7 or 8pm; in smaller towns they close at 2pm.

P

PHOTOGRAPHY and VIDEO (ΦΩΤΟΓΡΑΦΕΙΟ—*fotografío*)

Major brands of colour and black-and-white film are available, but prices are slightly higher than at home. Polaroid film is difficult to find. Film developing is also available, but it's best to bring your own film supplies and have it processed back home. The odd shop in major towns sells blank video tapes, but it's always safest to bring your own supply.

Hand-held photo equipment—but not tripods—may be used in museums and on archaeological sites, but you may have to pay a small fee. For security reasons, it is illegal to use a telephoto lens aboard an aircraft flying over Greece. Photography is forbidden around Iráklion airport, in the Soúda Bay area, and near police and military installations.

I'd like a roll of film for this camera.	**Tha íthela éna film giaftí ti michaní.**
black-and-white film	**asprómavro film**
colour prints	**énchromo film**
colour slides	**énchromo film giá sláïds**
35 mm film	**éna film triánda pénde milimétr**
How long will it take to develop (and print) this film?	**Se póses iméres boríte na emfanísete (ke na ektipósete) aftó to film?**
May I take a picture?	**Boró na páro mía fotografía?**
blank video tape	**miá vídeo-kasséta**

Crete

POLICE *(astinomía)* *(See also Emergencies on page 112)*

There are two kinds of police on Crete. The regular police *(chorofílakes)* wear green uniforms. The Tourist Police *(touristikí astinomía)* help visitors personally and also accompany state inspectors to hotels and restaurants to ensure that proper standards and prices are maintained. They wear national flag patches on their dark-grey uniforms to indicate the foreign languages they speak.

When on Crete, EU members have the same rights by law as any Greek citizen. Your consulate will be able to advise on legal matters.

The traffic police check car documents, operate speed traps and issue fines for illegal parking (fines in Greece are high).

Emergency number: **100**

Tourist Police: **171**, or

Iráklion: (081) 283190;	**Chaniá**: (0821) 45871;
Réthimnon: (0831) 28156;	**Ágios Nikólaos**: (0841) 26900

Where's the nearest police station? **Pou íne to kodinótero astinomikó tmíma?**

PUBLIC HOLIDAYS *(argíes)*
(See also Calendar of Events on page 89)

Banks, offices and shops are closed on the following national holidays, as well as during some feasts and festivals:

1 January	*Protochroniá*	New Year's Day
6 January	*ton Theofaníon*	Epiphany
25 March	*Ikostí Pémti Martíou (tou Evangelismoú)*	Greek Independence Day
1 May	*Protomagiá*	May Day
15 August	*Dekapendávgoustos (tis Panagías)*	Assumption Day
28 October	*Ikostí Ogdóï Oktovríou*	Óchi ("No") Day, commemorating Greek defiance of Italian invasion in 1940
25 December	*Christoúgenna*	Christmas Day
26 December	*Défteri iméra ton Christougénnon*	St. Stephen's Day

Movable dates	*Katharí Deftéra*	Clean Monday (First day of Lent)
	Megáli Paraskeví	Good Friday
	Deftéra tou Páscha	Easter Monday
	Análipsis	Ascension
	tou Agíou Pnévmatos	Whit Monday ("Holy Spirit")

Note: The dates on which the movable holy days are celebrated often differ from those in Catholic and Protestant countries.

Are you open tomorrow? **Échete aniktá ávrio?**

R

RELIGION

The island's faith is almost 100% Greek Orthodox. There are no Anglican or other Protestant services held, nor is there a Jewish congregation. Mass is said on Saturdays, Sundays and holy days at Catholic churches in Iráklion, Chaniá, Réthimnon, and Ágios Nikólaos.

T

TIME DIFFERENCES

The chart below shows the time difference between Greece and various cities. In summer, Greek clocks are put forward one hour.

	New York	London	**Crete**	Jo'burg	Sydney	Auckland
winter:	5am	10am	**noon**	noon	9pm	11pm
summer:	5am	10am	**noon**	11am	7pm	9pm

What time is it? **Ti óra íne?**

TIPPING

By law, service charges are included in the bill at hotels, restaurants and tavernas, but it is customary to leave a little more—unless, of course, the service has not been good. Some general guidelines:

Hotel porter	*100drs per bag*
Waiter	*5-10% (optional)*

123

Crete

Taxi drivers	*10% (optional, but customary)*
Tour guide (half-day)	*150-300drs (optional)*
Lavatory attendant	*50drs*

TOILETS/RESTROOMS (ΤΟΥΑΛΕΤΤΕΣ—*toaléttes*)

All towns of any size on the north coast have public toilets. Remember to leave a small tip if there is an attendant. In villages, try a café or taverna. If you drop in specifically to use the facilities, it is customary to have a drink before leaving. There are generally two doors, marked (ΓΥΝΑΙΚΩΝ) (ladies) and (ΑΝΔΡΩΝ) (gentlemen).

Note: If there's a waste bin, you're expected to put toilet tissue in that—not down the toilet. Toilets easily become clogged!

Where are the toilets?	**Pou íne i toualéttes?**

TOURIST INFORMATION OFFICES (*grafío pliroforión tourismoú*)

The Greek National Tourist Organization can provide assistance in preparing for your trip and while you are in Crete. They supply a range of colourful brochures and maps for the region in various languages and can generally give information on hotels, campsites and itineraries.

Australia: 51-57 Pitt Street, Sydney, NSW 2000; tel. (02) 241-1663.
Canada: 1300 Bay Street, Toronto, Ont. M5R 3K8, tel. (416) 968-2220; 1233 rue de la Montagne, Montréal, Que. H3G 1Z2, tel. (514) 871-1535.
UK: 4 Conduit Street, London W1R 0DJ, tel. (0171) 734-5997.
USA: 645 5th Avenue, New York, NY 10022, tel. (212) 421-5777; 611 W. 6th Street, Los Angeles, CA 90017, tel. (213) 626-6696; 168 N. Michigan Avenue, Chicago, IL 60601, tel. (312) 782-1084.

In the main towns on Crete, the tourist information offices are signposted EOT (*Ellinikós Organismós Tourismoú*).

Iráklion: across from Archaeological Museum at Xanthoudidou 1, tel. (081) 228203, open 8am-2:30pm.
Chaniá: Odos Kriari 40 (4th floor), off Platía 1866, tel. (0821) 92943, open 8am-2pm and 3pm-8:30pm.
Réthimnon: Venizelou 20, tel. (0831) 21143, open 8am-2:30pm Monday to Friday.

Ágios Nikólaos: Akti Koundouron 20 on the quay where the lake joins the harbour, tel. (0841) 22357, open 8:30am-10pm Monday to Friday.

Where's the tourist office?   **Pou íne to grafío tourismoú?**

TRANSPORT (See also Planning Your Budget on page 119)

Buses (leoforío). In general, Crete's buses are dependable and punctual. Besides the frequent services connecting Iráklion, Ágios Nikólaos, Réthimnon, and Chaniá, buses also serve all the archaeological sites and most of the island's villages. When using buses for the more remote excursions into the countryside, be sure to check times of the return trip. Be punctual, as buses sometimes arrive (and leave) slightly early! You can buy tickets in advance at the bus stations in main towns, or on the bus. Hold on to them in case inspectors board the bus to check.

For city buses around Iráklion and Chaniá and to Knossós, buy tickets in advance from kiosks.

Taxis (ΤΑΞΙ—taxí). Taxis are reasonably cheap on Crete. The drivers are generally helpful and honest, although many in Iráklion are more calculating. It's cheaper to flag a taxi down on the road; there is a surcharge for calling one.

Town taxis operate with a meter, which in the daytime should be set to "1" ("2" is the double fare for night hours, midnight-5am). If there is no meter, agree on a fare before setting off. Fares to various destinations are often posted at taxi ranks and airports. It is perfectly legitimate for a surcharge to be added at Easter and Christmas, as well as for luggage and late-night trips. Rounding up the fare is the usual way of tipping, with a little extra for special services rendered.

In the main towns, taxis are plentiful, both cruising and at taxi ranks, usually near the port or the bus station. Almost every village has at least one taxi. These rural taxis are called agoréon. It can be worth hiring a taxi for a half-day or day excursion, or pre-arranging for one to pick you up from a site or village, particularly if there are several of you to share the cost. But always agree a price in advance.

Ferries and boats. Small boats can be hired at most resort areas for sightseeing along the coast and day trips to secluded beaches and outlying islands. You should be experienced with boats before taking one out on your own, however.

Crete

For ferries to Santorini and other Greek islands, there are numerous travel agents in main towns and resorts who can advise you. The major ferry lines have representatives all along 25 Avgoústou Street in Iráklion. There are ports at Iráklion, Chaniá, Sitía and other towns.

What's the fare to…?	**Piá íne i timí giá…?**
When's the next bus to…?	**Póte févgi to epómeno leoforío giá…?**
single (one-way)	**apló**
return (round-trip)	**me epistrofí**

TRAVELLERS WITH DISABILITIES

Crete has not yet properly geared up its tourist facilities for assisting travellers with disabilities. Some hotels are adapting their amenities, but it is a slow process and you should inquire ahead of time about precisely what is available.

The mountainous terrain of the interior is a major obstacle for getting around. Check with tour operators at home to see if their tours are suitable, or if special ones are offered for people with disabilities. Be sure to bring any medicines you might need and a medical certificate with you.

TRAVELLING TO CRETE *(See also Airports on page 102)*

By air

International flights. Most scheduled flights to Crete go via Athens. Olympic Airways operates daily between Athens and Chaniá or Iráklion, each about a 45-minute trip.

From the U.K. and Ireland. There is a wide selection of package tours and seat-only flights to Crete, from April to October. Prices vary according to tour operator, time of travel and the kind of accommodation. Most travel agents recommend cancellation insurance, and some tour operators require personal insurance as well.

From North America. Economical charter flights are arranged by clubs or associations for members and immediate families. Also try your travel agent for tour operators' packages to Crete. Various airlines offer services to Athens from New York, Boston, and Montréal. Another option is to fly via a European gateway city, such as London, and pick up a connecting or charter flight there.

By rail

The most direct route passes through Paris and Berne to Italy (Brindisi or Ancona), where you get the ferry to mainland Greece (the ferry crossing is often included in the fare). From there you can catch a ferry on to Crete.

For European residents, Inter-Rail tickets are valid in Greece. Non-European residents can travel on an unlimited-mileage Eurailpass ticket, valid for travel in throughout western Europe. You must sign up before leaving home.

By road

Because of poor road conditions and ongoing conflict in parts of the in former Yugoslavia, it is no longer recommended to make the journey from northern Europe to Greece by road. You can, however, drive through France and Italy and catch an Italy–Greece ferry. Advance booking is recommended.

Some coach operators offer trips from London and continental Europe to Athens, where you can catch a flight or ferry to Crete.

By sea

Most travellers use the ferries from Italy to the Greek mainland. The main Adriatic port is Brindisi, with less frequent services from Bari and Venice. Luxury boats leave from Ancona, and there is also a direct service from there to Iráklion.

During peak season, there are many sailings each week and a daily car ferry from Piraeus to Iráklion (12 hours) and Chaniá (11 hours). Along with Sitía and Ágios Nikólaos, these ports have services to and from the Aegean islands, principally Rhodes, Santorini (Thíra) ,and Mykonos.

W

WATER (neró)

Tap water is almost always safe to drink, but may have a high mineral content. Bottled water is also widely available.

Most hotels have solar panels that provide the hot water supply, and those in the lower price ranges may run out on cloudy days or if there are many guests. The best time to be sure of a hot shower is 4-7pm. Always use water conservatively to help prevent shortages on this dry island.

Crete

Santa Marina Beach Hotel ✪✪ *Amoudára (Iráklion region) Tel. (081) 261103; fax (081) 261369.* Large, comfortable modern hotel, 6 km (4 miles) from the centre of Iráklion. Lovely grounds along wide, sandy beach. 210 rooms with air-conditioning, refrigerator. Restaurant, snack bar, swimming pool, tennis, playground, games room, watersports, parking.

CENTRAL CRETE

El Greco Hotel ✪ *Agía Galíni. Tel. (0832) 91187; fax (0832) 91491.* Bright, modern hotel with great sea views over the harbour. Bar, breakfast room. 16 rooms.

Idi Hotel ✪ *Zarós (Iráklion region). Tel. (0894) 31301; fax (0894) 31511.* An oasis of quiet in the foothills of Mount Ida, ideal for mountain excursions. Beautiful grounds with swimming pool, working water mill, trout farm, and restaurant. 35 rooms. Open all year.

Stelios Rooms ✪ *Agía Galíni. Tel. (0832) 91383; fax (0832) 91030.* Small but comfortable establishment. Rooms with balconies overlooking the sea. 23 rooms.

EASTERN CRETE
Hersónissos

Antinoös ✪✪ *Limín Hersónissou. Tel. (0897) 23142.* Surprisingly tasteful. 29 rooms, two minutes east of town.

Creta Maris ✪✪✪ *Limín Hersónissou. Tel. (0897) 22115; fax (0897) 22130.* Giant modern hotel complex. 516 rooms, many in tasteful bungalows, small private beach, two minutes from public beach, tennis, swimming pool and live music.

Ágios NikÓlaos/ EloÚnda

Akti Olous ✪✪ *Eloúnda. Tel. (0841) 41270; fax (0841) 41425.* Modern hotel on the beach below town, with a superb view of the bay. Restaurant, bar, roof garden, swimming pool, watersports.

Ariadne Beach ✪✪ *Ágios Nikólaos. Tel. (0841) 22741; fax (0841) 22005.* Pretty setting in landscaped gardens with private beach. 76 rooms and bungalows, swimming pool and good sports facilities.

Elounda Marc ✪✪✪ *Eloúnda. Tel. (0841) 41102; fax (0841) 41307.* One of the first hotels in Greece is set on the sea in vast gardens. Many of the lodgings are in bungalows with private swimming pools. 95 rooms, 3 restaurants, beach, watersports.

Sofia ✪ *Eloúnda. Tel. (0841) 41482; fax (0841) 41034.* Pleasant, friendly, and inexpensive pension in town.

Sitía

Elysée ✪ *14 Karamánli Street, Sitía. Tel. (0843) 22312; fax (0843) 23427.* 24 modern, comfortable rooms, each with refrigerator. Seafront location, near beach. Good value.

Itanos Hotel ✪ *Sitía. Tel. (0843) 22146; fax (0843) 22915.* Basic but pleasant hotel situated on the central seaside square. 77 rooms with balconies, some facing waterfront. Restaurant, bar, cafeteria. Open all year.

WESTERN CRETE

Réthimnon

Atlantis Beach Hotel ✪✪✪ *26 Ari Velouhioti. Tel. (0831) 23517; fax (0831) 51068.* Lovely A-class hotel on Réthimnon's sandy beach, 1.5 km (1 mile) from town centre. 90 comfortable rooms with air-conditioning and balconies overlooking the sea or the hotel gardens. Good service, lounge, bar, restaurant, snack bar, swimming pool, tennis, games room, playground.

Crete

Ideon Hotel ✪✪ *10 N. Plastira Square. Tel. (0831) 28667; fax (0831) 28670.* Pleasant, modern and comfortable establishment overlooking waterfront in the old town. Swimming pool, lounge, restaurant. 90 rooms with balcony.

Palazzo Rimondi ✪✪✪ *21 Xanthoudidou. Tel. (0831) 51289; fax (0831) 26757.* pleasant suites, all with kitchens, occupy several 15th-century houses in the old quarter. Swimming pool and bar.

Chaniá

Amphora ✪✪ *20 Parodos Theotokopoúlos. Tel./fax (0821) 93224.* Charming old 14th-century mansion—the prettiest building on the harbour front. 14 rooms, 10 minutes from beach, restaurant. Open all year.

Casa Delfino ✪✪✪ *9 Theofanous. Tel. (0821) 93098; fax (0821) 96500.* 12 smartly furnished, air-conditioned studios in an exquisite 17th-century Venetian mansion in the centre of the old town.

Doma ✪✪✪ *124 Eleftherion Venizelon. Tel. (0821) 51772; fax (0821) 41578.* A 19th-century seaside mansion, once a consulate, is filled with antiques; 10-minute walk to old quarter. Excellent rooftop restaurant. 25 rooms. Closed Nov-March.

El Greco ✪ *49 Theotokopoúlos Street. Tel. (0821) 90432; fax (0821) 91829.* Basic rooms in a picturesque, vine-covered building in the old town. 26 rooms, breakfast room, roof garden with harbour views.

Porto Veneziano ✪✪✪ *Palio Limani, Chaniá. Tel. (0821) 27100; fax (0821) 27105.* A modern hotel, with excellent sea views and unusually stylish, comfortable rooms, at the end of the inner harbour, 57 rooms, near the old quarter and 10 minutes from beach. Open all year.

Recommended Restaurants

Throughout Crete, you can eat well in modest little tavernas at very reasonable prices. In the larger towns and resorts, you'll find a range of restaurants catering for the tourist trade, as well as a few upmarket establishments serving international cuisine.

Reservations are only advisable for top restaurants in high season. Some restaurants close one day a week, which may vary in and out of season, and others are open only in the evening, so telephone first to confirm.

Restaurant prices, like the dishes served, are fairly consistent across the island. A small cover charge of 100-200drs is standard. Service is included in the bill, but it's customary to leave a bit more. The price guidelines below are per person, for a two-course meal including cover and house wine or beer; expect to pay more for fresh fish, which is generally expensive.

✪	under 3,000 drachmas
✪✪	over 3,000 drachmas

IRÁKLION

Bougátsa Kirkor ✪ *Venizélou Square, by the fountain. No telephone.* The best place to sample Crete's traditional *bougátsa*, a hot cheesy pastry sprinkled with sugar and cinnamon.

Dore ✪✪ *Eleftherías Square (lift in arcade). Tel. (081) 225212.* Romantic, fifth-floor roof garden restaurant with lovely views over the city and harbour.

Giovanni ✪✪ *12 Korai. Tel. (081) 246338.* Classy restaurant serving upmarket Greek dishes, steaks, and fish. Good wine list.

Ippokampos ✪ *Mitsotaki and 25 Avgoústou Street. Tel. (081) 280240.* This traditional *oúzeri* near the Venetian harbour serves good, inexpensive seafood and Greek specialities. Especially popular with the locals.

Crete

Loukoulos ✪✪ *5 Korai. Tel. (081) 224435.* Stylish restaurant serving fine Italian cuisine and Greek dishes.

CENTRAL CRETE

Horiatis Taverna ✪ *Agía Galíni. No telephone.* Authentic Greek cooking served in an unusual little stone taverna.

Kronio ✪ *Izermiado (on Lasithi Plateau). Tel. (0844) 22375.* Home cooking in charming family-run establishment.

La Strada Restaurant ✪✪ *Agía Galíni. Tel. (0832) 91053.* Excellent pizza cooked in a wood-fired oven. Roof garden, friendly coffee bar and a long list of wines.

EASTERN CRETE

Ágios NikÓláos

Creta Restaurant ✪✪ *Koundourou Street, Agios Nikólaos. Tel. (0841) 31726.* Harbourside restaurant serving international and Greek food.

Ithanos ✪ *Platia Iroon, Agios Nikólaos. Tel. (0841) 25340.* Popular with locals, who enjoy *soutzoukakia* (meatballs) and other traditional dishes.

Pelagos ✪✪ *Koraka Street, Agios Nikólaos. behind the tourist office. No telephone.* Cheerful restaurant with a wooden fishing boat out front. Fresh fish and Cretan dishes. Evenings only.

EloÚnda

Ferryman Taverna ✪-✪✪ *On the waterfront, Eloúnda. Tel. (0841) 41230.* Excellent Greek cooking, served with a flare! Try the fish soup and the traditional pork speciality with apples, sultanas, cheese and ham.

Marilena ✪ *On the waterfront. No telephone.* Wonderful appetizers and other dishes, served in a garden.

Nikos ✪ *On the central square, Eloúnda. No telephone.* Very pleasant taverna where fish is recommended.